Above : Running into the sunlight. "Victor Wild" at Potters Bar, another study by George Heiron.

Below : The Côte du Nord in Brittany, a picture made a few days before the line closed in 1959.

WORLD OF
MODEL RAILWAYS

By JOSEPH MARTIN

Illustrations by R. M. Schofield

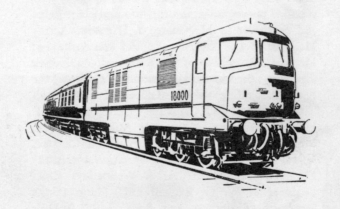

PERCIVAL MARSHALL
1960

GRATEFUL ACKNOWLEDGMENTS

Frank Norris's *The Octopus*, an incident in which suggested the story of Dyke's ride, may now be obtained as a paperback (Bantam Books). The publishers of Kipling (page 3) and Hugh Walpole (page 4) are Macmillan and Co., and the poetry of W. H. Auden, from whose "Night Mail" four lines are quoted on page 4, is published by Faber and Faber. The author and publishers of *The World of Model Railways* gratefully acknowledge the quotations. They also express their thanks to those who supplied photographs, information and other help; and especially to Mr George J. Handzik, Acting Manager of The Atchison, Topeka and Santa Fe; Mr A. C. Kalmbach of the Kalmbach Publishing Company; the Lionel Corporation of America; the Franklin Institute; the Press Officers of the Pennsylvania Railroad and Canadian Pacific; Mr C. M. Mitchell, Director of the City Museum, Leeds; Mr Jack Dove, Borough Librarian and Curator, Hove; Mr F. Riley, Editor of *Meccano Magazine*; Mr Neill Perrin; Mr A. J. Webberley, Chief Designer of W. G. Bagnall Ltd., Stafford; the Secretary of Peckett and Sons, Ltd., Bristol; Mr Martin Evans and Mr Robin Orchard of *Model Engineer*; and Mr R. E. Dock, Editor of *Model Railway News*.

PRINTED AND MADE IN GREAT BRITAIN BY
FLETCHER AND SON LTD NORWICH AND
THE LEIGHTON-STRAKER BOOKBINDING CO LTD LONDON

CONTENTS

TO ALL THE FATHERS
WHO *LIKE* TO HELP

Do you remember it as I remember,
A Christmas morning long ago?
The thin dawn-light of late December,
Crackle of paper, an exploring toe—

And then the certainty: a box is resting,
Smooth-wrapped and heavy on the bed;
The eager foot withdraws from questing,
Its message thrilled to the half-dreaming head.

Investigating toes need not be clever
To know what *this* box must contain.
Promised the "grandest Christmas ever",
A boy is sleeping; at his feet a Train.

CHAPTER ONE

The Thrill of Railways

AS Dyke galloped towards the railway station his pursuers began to close in on him. Three men from the ranch were riding down to cut him off when he reached the road, and behind him the sheriff and his posse were dangerously close. Rising in his saddle, he saw a cloud of dust and the flash of gun-barrels in the sun.

Suddenly his eyes fell upon an engine steaming quietly by itself on the up-line. With the roll of hooves growing louder, he sprang from his horse and jumped, pistol in hand, for the cab. Two men on the engine tumbled off quickly. He reached for the levers. There was a hiss of steam and the great engine trembled with

power. The driving wheels turned slowly, slipped, spun, and then gripped the rails just as a shot smashed the cab window.

Gathering speed, the locomotive rolled out of the station and into the open country. Dyke knew that he must make the most of his head-

His eyes fell upon an engine steaming quietly by . . . .

start. Smoke poured in black clouds from the stack and every joint shuddered with the strain.

Farther along the line were special points, put there so that a runaway engine could be swung off the main line before it crashed into something. The sheriff remembered these points and ran for the telegraph office. He yelled an order to the clerk: "Wire ahead to open the switch at Pixley. We'll derail him there!"

Then he raced to an engine which was standing in the station at the head of a goods train. "'Name of the State of California!" he shouted. Without stopping to ask questions, the engine driver and fireman uncoupled the locomotive. The sheriff and his men crowded into the cab and were soon flying after Dyke—on the downline, so that the two engines were thundering in the same direction on different tracks.

Having thrown everything wide open, Dyke leaned on his elbow at the window. The wind roared past his face as he looked back and saw the other engine in wild pursuit. Pulling the fire-door ajar, he stoked vigorously for a few moments.

The hand of the steam indicator was rising when he spotted a signal set at "Danger" where a line branched off. He knew what it meant. The sheriff had been quick-witted enough to think of the switch, but he had not known, or had forgotten, that it was connected with a signal which worked automatically to warn any driver who might be approaching.

Dyke had no course but to go back: it was the lesser of the two dangers. Slowing speed, he prepared to reverse. The wheels slid, the cab shook, and the engine strained gradually backwards.

Leaving the controls, Dyke took grim hold of his revolver. He was travelling fast again, and his pursuers were still rocking madly along the parallel track. Soon the engines would pass. When they were still two hundred yards apart, the firing began. They passed in a roar and tumult. Voices yelled through the steam and smoke, bullets clanged on metal, and splinters of wood and glass whizzed through the air. Dyke emptied his revolver. The blue smoke from gunpowder curled upwards and mingled with the black smoke from the engine.

Dyke felt a sharp pain and knew that a bullet must have grazed his hip. He had no time to worry about it. Nor could he bother much about the other engine, now trying to check its headlong dash. All that mattered to him was that he still had a chance of reaching the mountains. He was not going to surrender. Putting on speed, he tore back towards the station at the risk of being shot, for more men were waiting there. He hurtled through a storm of bullets; and not one of them found its mark.

Free for a while, he roared over a wooden bridge and out on to the prairie where the wheat spread around him like an ocean …

You can read of Dyke's adventures in *The Octopus* by Frank Norris. Railways play an exciting part in the stories of the Wild West. They thrill us again when we follow the exploits of Wells Fargo, or of William Cody, who earned his nickname of Buffalo Bill by selling buffalo meat to the railroad builders; and there is often a train to keep us on tiptoe in the tales by Zane Grey, the former New York dentist whose Westerns had sold more than twenty-five million copies at the time of his death.

Some of the events which really happened were as exciting as any of the invented stories on television. In England, even when railways were no longer new, train travellers sometimes made their will before they left on a journey; and in America until a much later date they

He was travelling fast again …

took a gun with them and kept it within quick reach. Trouble was caused by outlaws and bandits as well as by the hostile Indians, who can hardly be blamed for not liking their hunting grounds to be invaded. "The bad men died with their boots on", said the police chief of the Union Pacific.

American railway thrills were not confined to the West. If you have seen Walt Disney's film *The Great Locomotive Chase* you will know about the Andrews Raid: how a party of Northern soldiers disguised as civilians ran off with the *General* at Big Shanty in Georgia during the Civil War and were chased by another engine—much as Dyke was in the story—for eighty-seven rip-roaring miles. Both locomotives still exist, as showpieces: the *General* at Union Station in Chattanooga and the *Texas* at the Cyclorama in Atlanta. Their places were taken in the film by two engines which were still working well, the *William Mason* of 1856 and the Baldwin *Inyo* of 1875. The *Inyo* was built to help carry the great consignment of silver from the Comstock Lode near Virginia City in Nevada, and I shall not be surprised if a new film is soon made about this engine too—with bandits after the silver!

One of the most thrilling train journeys in fiction contains nothing of this sort, no robbers, no Indians, no pursuits, and no monkey tricks such as crashing rocks on to the line. You will find it in Rudyard Kipling's *Captains Courageous*. Kipling tells of a pampered boy, the son of very rich parents, who is washed off a liner, picked up in the fog by some fishermen, and forced to stay on board the schooner until the end of the cod-fishing: an experience which does him a world of good. As radio has not yet been invented (the book was first published in 1897) Mr and Mrs Cheyne do not know for six months that Harvey is alive. Mr Cheyne is far away from the port where the schooner has put in—but he owns a railway, and so you can guess what happens:

*Los Angeles called to San Diego and Barstow that the Southern California engineers might know and be ready in their lonely round-houses; Barstow passed the word to the Atlantic and Pacific; and Albuquerque flung it the whole length of the Atchison, Topeka, and Santa Fe management, even into Chicago. An engine, combination-car with crew, and the great and gilded "Constance" private car were to be "ex-*pedited" over those two thousand three hundred and fifty miles. The train would take precedence of one hundred and seventy-seven others meeting and passing; despatchers and crews of every one of those said trains must be notified. Sixteen locomotives, sixteen engineers, and sixteen firemen would be needed—each and every one the best available. Two and one-half minutes would be allowed for changing engines; three for watering and two for coaling.*

What a ride! "The needle of the speed indicator flicked to and fro; the cinders rattled on the roof, and a whirl of dust sucked after the whirling wheels. Now they looked out into great abysses, a trestle purring beneath their tread, or up to rocks that barred out half the stars." This is exactly as it would have been. I have made such a journey, over prairies and through mountains and forests, half-a-dozen times—though not in such a hurry. I used to wish that I was with Mr Cheyne in his emergency. If you feel like this when you read *Captains Courageous* it may interest you that "a real live railway magnate", as Kipling called him, was stirred so much by Mr Cheyne's wild dash that he called out his own engines and men, hitched on his private car, and dashed along the same route. Kipling always took great pains with the facts in his fiction and he invented the ride from expert information. Knowing that the journey could be accomplished, the railway magnate set out to beat Mr Cheyne's time. He deservedly succeeded.

Everywhere trains are associated with thrills. Have you ever thought how many adventures in fiction begin with a railway journey? In *The Thirty-Nine Steps* strange things happen to Richard Hannay while he is in London, but we know that the dangers are going to increase when the Galloway train carries him slowly across the moors and he steps out at a quiet little place where the stationmaster is digging potatoes in his garden. John Buchan's characters travel a good deal by rail; *Mr Standfast* opens with men in a railway carriage.

Few of us are ever involved in dangerous adventures such as came the way of Richard Hannay. But the railway often provides us with quieter thrills of the sort that we enjoy, not in the pages of John Buchan and Zane Grey, but in the school stories by Hugh Walpole when Jeremy travels down to Glebeshire (or Cornwall) for his summer holidays. We all know the fun and excitement of catching the train and finding seats, of watching the towns and villages slip by, of seeing the landscape change and even the style of the houses. Finally, we have the happiness of arriving, perhaps in the sunny evening calm. Our trip may involve a branch line like the one which takes Jeremy on his last lap to the sea: "The train arriving at last, they all climbed into it, and then had to wait for a hot, grilling half-hour whilst the engine made up its mind that it was worth its while to take all the trouble to start off again."

It is partly because we associate trains with holidays, with leisure and freedom and the sparkle and smell of the sea, that we are so fond of them. But trains and railways are also exciting for their own sake. Whenever a locomotive appears on the screen, even if only for a few moments—just drawing into a station, or pulling away, or rounding a curve—we take notice at once. There is something about a train that stirs us. Who can fail to be moved by the sight and sound of a night express as it thunders past? The night mail is particularly grand:

Pulling up Beattock, a steady climb—
The gradient's against her but she's on time.

Past cotton grass and moorland boulder,
Shovelling white steam over her shoulder.

Nor is this all. There is romance in the ordinary operations of a railway. "Romance brought up the nine-fifteen." The arranging and planning of trains, the running to timetable, the signalling and shunting, the working of points: all these operations, and many others, are endlessly interesting. No one enjoys them more than the owner of a model railway. He controls the whole system. Like an enormous giant, he has a complete world literally at his finger-tips. Whatever he chooses to do, nobody will write to the newspapers complaining that a train is always late or over-crowded!

In the following pages I shall try to show you some of the fascination of running your own trains. As a true model takes its meaning from the larger thing that it represents, I constantly relate the miniature railway to the big one, for this is the best and obvious way of explaining the sense and purpose of our work.

The beginner is guided to a point where he is not quite a beginner any more. A few parts, and particularly those concerned with electricity and scale, will probably be more helpful to the co-operating father than to the boy of ten or eleven; but the boy may turn back to them later, for a closer study, when he and the railway have grown. A view over the horizon should encourage him.

Nothing here is very difficult. Indeed, I have taken the risk of occasionally being too simple for some in order that the greater number may benefit. At the same time, there are no sudden gaps or neat side-steps to make the hard look easy. Not long ago I read an article explaining a conjuring trick for boys. It was all beautifully simple until one came to almost the last sentence: "Unknown to the audience, you have slipped the other cards to the back of your hand." It seemed to me that the article was itself a conjuring trick! Anyway, there is no sleight-of-hand in this book; whatever its faults, it can at least claim to be straightforward. We run on a smooth track, and I think that you will pick up a number of useful bits-and-pieces on the way.

Let's clear the line, then. Romance brings up the nine-fifteen!

CHAPTER TWO

Better Than Ever

ON my first visit to Washington I spent an afternoon at the National Museum which is part of the great Smithsonian Institution. The Land Transportation Building was trembling under one of its August invasions by schoolboys from all points of the compass. One of the newest and largest things which they could see was a modern rocket. Did they crowd in front of it wide-eyed? Not at all; they each stopped for a couple of seconds and then hurried off. They were eager to look at exhibits of more interest not far away: the railway engines and models, rather like those at the Science Museum in London.

We live in an age of atomic and electronic wonders, of space rockets and radio-telescopes, of calculating machines that appear to think and aircraft that fly faster than sound. Yet the locomotive is a greater favourite than ever before. A railway engine does not astonish us as do some of the latest devices in science; it does not take off for the Moon or Mars; it is not even new. But none of this matters. An engine is closer to our daily living than a moon rocket. Though it is not mechanically simple (it may have 25,000 moving parts) we can understand it as we are unable to understand many of the new scientific inventions. It is something that we know and like. Few of us can feel much fondness for a computer however wonderful it may be!

There are now more railway lovers of all kinds than there were in the days when the train was the only means of travelling fast. The biggest increase is among the operators of model layouts. Their numbers rose after the war and then began to shoot up amazingly. How can we explain this? Some may reply that boys have more pocket-money nowadays and can therefore build up an interesting model railway in a fairly short time. But the increase is by no means confined to boys; the average age of enthusiasts on both sides of the Atlantic is thirty-four. Obviously, then, we must look for other reasons.

During the war thousands of men learnt to make things in factories and Service workshops, and in prisoner-of-war camps where an old rusty razor blade, a jagged piece of tin, or an odd bit of glass would be a secret and precious tool. When the war ended, this desire to make things—usually small things—often remained. Glad to be home, the men settled down as soon as possible to the comforts of a smaller and quieter world. Many of them, having more spare time and more money than before, decided to take up a hobby, one that would fit pleasantly into the home and also give them a chance to design and construct in a small space.

Besides answering these requirements, the model railway had the great advantage of being already familiar. Most men had owned a miniature layout in their earlier years. They remembered this when they looked into the model shop windows (frequently at the suggestion of a young son) and they realized almost with surprise that as grown-up men, no longer limited by a few pennies a week pocket-money, they

The Rainbow Train.

could build the railway which they would have loved to build when they were younger. Quite often a partnership was formed; father and son worked together, enjoying a project which they could share fully and happily.

We have explained the attraction of the hobby just after the war. But why should it be so very popular at present? There are again several reasons. One of them, of course, is the progress made in previous years. Once the hobby had become well established by the early 1950s, it was not likely to lose its hold for at least a few years. Meanwhile the manufacturers were turning out more and better trains, more and better equipment, and kits for beginner and expert alike. With smart model shops in almost every town, the hobby became increasingly attractive to the outsider—if any man is ever completely an outsider to model railways.

At the same time the Do-It-Yourself movement was growing, particularly among men who could easily develop an enthusiasm for constructing in scale miniature. Do-It-Yourself is absorbing and profitable, but there comes a time when the amateur craftsman has made pretty well everything that the home reasonably needs. He can hardly go on for the rest of his life producing shelves, cabinets, coffee tables and lampshades! Before the family moves out to make room for the furniture and gadgets, he turns to another hobby; and in model railway building he has one that may satisfy him. He can use his hands, his tools, and the skill which was improved on his other work, and he can practice the hobby in his home.

We are also being joined by some of the refugees from television; for when families tire of the television screen, when they no longer sit through a programme whether they like it or not, they still want something that will occupy them indoors. Evenings at home are now a custom in the towns as they always were in the country.

We hear it said that television is making us depend too much on entertainment provided by others. But something quite the opposite is happening. When the television set has ceased to be new and thrilling, the members of the family soon discover that there are other pleasures to be enjoyed in the home. They play their own games instead of watching the parlour games on the screen. They discuss all kinds of subjects, they read, and they interest themselves in various pastimes. It may be that we are returning to the home-life of our grandparents who played instruments, sang songs, painted pictures and generally made their own fun. In all this, the little railway has an honourable part to play, and is indeed already playing it.

The progress achieved by the hobby in the years from 1946 to 1952 is now benefiting a fresh generation of boys. For them the model railway is more exciting than it was for those who grew up before the war. I do not mean that the miniature trains of thirty years ago were poor and dull. At their best, they reached a very high standard. The leading makers were producing solid, honest work—which is why they are still leading makers—and nothing pleased a boy more than to receive a train set or accessories at Christmas.

Even at that period, the model train and model locomotive had a long history. If you visit the Science Museum at South Kensington you may see a miniature locomotive which is older than any full-sized engine of its kind in the world. Richard Trevithick made it in 1797 as one of the steps towards the historic engine that ran at Camborne in Cornwall on the wet Christmas Eve of 1801. Still earlier, William Murdoch constructed a couple of engines small enough to be tried in his room at Redruth—the next town to Camborne—before he experimented on the church path, much to the alarm of the parson.

The first railway engine to travel with smooth wheels on smooth rails was also a model, built by William Hedley who went on to construct the famous *Puffing Billy*. Rather similarly, before there was a proper steam railway in America old John Stevens was driving a small

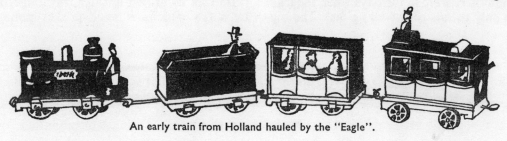

An early train from Holland hauled by the "Eagle".

engine on a track in his garden at Hoboken, across the Hudson River from New York. He had built it himself at the age of seventy-six after trying for many years to make the public understand what steam could do.

These engines were all made for serious experimental purposes. The real trains had to be running before small copies of them were made for pleasure. Most of the oldest models in our museums belong to the later years of the nineteenth century when the railway was solidly established. The boys of that time could buy an engine and tender for a penny, or build one with a wooden kit. Examples of both are to be seen among the fifteen hundred toys in the Kirkstall Abbey Museum at Leeds. The penny toy represents an engine and tender of about 1870, and the construction kit dates from about 1885. A more ambitious toy, believed to have been made in the early 1870s, shows an engine, tender and seven coaches with a dozen passengers inside, the whole standing on a tree-lined track thirty inches long. A gayer train could hardly be imagined. The coaches are royal blue and orange, dark blue and pink, orange and green, green and purple, salmon pink and dark green, plain green, and plain mauve; and a pattern of daisies is painted on for further decoration. What a surprise for morning travellers if the 8.16 turned up in these colours!

Mr R. West, who lives at Wilton in Northamptonshire, has a little engine of the 1840s, with reversing gear, cylinder exhaust through the chimney, a water tank in the tender, proper springs, axle-boxes which take grease, and cab levers, brakes and whistle; all made by hand, at $\frac{3}{8}$ in. to the foot, from solid brass. This is much closer to being a work of art than the average engine or train which exists from the same period. Already at this early stage we have on one hand the simple toy, delightful for a small child and on the other hand the toy which is first cousin to a model.

Trains of these two kinds continued to be produced for many years and are still produced to-day, the simple ones for the toddler and the better ones for the child who is nearly ready for clockwork. The wooden trains of the last century were always charming and sometimes beautiful. A museum in Holland has an odd-looking little green engine named *Eagle* with a green open wagon and two carriages, one of them yellow and the other yellow and black.

Figures represent the driver and passengers. One man sits in the open third-class wagon, which resembles a tender, and another (possibly the guard) has a fine view from the top of the last carriage.

Miniature trains were also constructed of metal. Long ago a set of this kind found its way to a toyshop in an out-of-the-way Irish village. The engine *Noris* and the tender, passenger coach and goods truck (which has a rail at the sides) are of $\frac{7}{8}$ in. gauge with an overall length of $8\frac{3}{4}$ in. They now have a safe resting-place in Hove Museum.

Railway toys and models helped to make the public friendlier towards steam travel. In George Stephenson's time the railway had many enemies. Owners of country estates, wanting the steam highway to keep well away from their parks and pheasants, spread all sorts of tales, or made the most of ignorant beliefs which were common, such as that, if trains were allowed to run, cows would cease to give milk, hens would stop laying, birds would suffocate and children would be stricken with terror. But the ghastly train looked anything but ghastly when it was seen in miniature; on the

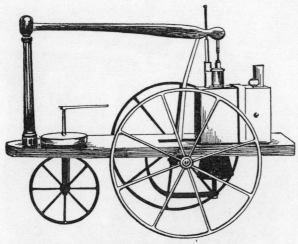

William Murdoch's engine.

contrary, it was a lovable thing which instantly appealed to children. Without doubt, the railways owe a good deal to the tiny copies of themselves. This fact has long been recognized, and the men operating our railways are always keen to assist those who pursue the hobby or have a keen general interest in trains. How often have we seen a picture of an engine-driver chatting from his cab to a schoolboy on the platform?

The peoples of the world all have their own customs and habits. Great differences exist even within the same nation. If you are Scottish you probably like salt porridge and the music of bagpipes; if you are English, Welsh or Irish you probably dislike at least one of them. Much greater differences are found when one crosses the Channel. But they are small compared with those between countries which are far apart in position, climate and history. French frogs and snails would seem to you a less strange food after you had travelled in distant lands and been offered bird's-nest soup or a dish of spiders. More surprising still would be many of the other likings and customs which you encountered. In Tibet you would meet people who covered themselves with fat instead of washing and in Persia people who did not wash because of their great reverence for water.

However surprising or startling these contrasts may be, we can always be sure that a miniature train will be liked everywhere. Set one going in a shop window of any town or city and very few people will walk straight past. Wind up a clockwork one in a village of New Guinea, or of the Matto Grosso in Brazil where Colonel Fawcett disappeared, and the natives are immediately fascinated. Knowing this, more than one explorer has packed a clockwork set with the mirrors and gramophone which are White Man's Magic in primitive parts of the world. Few explorers can "arrange" an eclipse of the sun or moon as Sir Henry Curtis and his companions did in *King Solomon's Mines*, but anyone can wind up the clockwork motor of a gramophone or model locomotive!

Again and again the miniature train has been used as an instrument of friendship, a present that was bound to please. In 1852, when Japan was still a secret country remote from the rest of the world, President Millard Fillmore of the United States sent a letter to the Emperor suggesting that the country should be opened up to Western trade. The letter was delivered by Matthew Calbraith Perry, a famous sailor who had been a midshipman at fifteen and had later commanded the first American warship to be driven by steam. Commodore Perry took with him, as gifts from the President, a miniature engine, tender, passenger coach and track, together with a lineside telegraph. Astonished and delighted, the Japanese watched the train running at twenty miles an hour; and they were also amazed to discover that the telegraph "spoke" Japanese as easily as English and Dutch.

An agreement was signed between the two countries just when some of the Japanese noblemen wanted all foreigners within their borders to be killed. While I will not say that Commodore Perry's train led directly to the treaty which made Japan part of the modern world, it undoubtedly helped to create the right feeling. Not only did it please the Japanese and thus add to the friendliness of the meeting; it showed them, at the same time, two wonders which belonged to the Western nations and could be brought to Japan. As the result of that treaty, Japan soon became a busy manufacturing country. Goods from her factories were sent all over the world, and the best-known of them, next perhaps to cotton dresses, were cheap toys. If you saw a child playing with a brightly-coloured engine there was a good chance that it bore the words *Made in Japan*. Commodore Perry's train had come back, so to speak, a million times over!

The pleasure which the American train gave to the Emperor of Japan has been enjoyed by rulers in many other countries. While touring the United States as an official guest, Nikita

Kruschev complained almost with tears that the security men would not let him visit Walt Disney's railway wonderland. Maharajahs, rajahs, emirs, sultans, pashas and sheikhs have a great fondness for model railway systems, and more than once an S.O.S. has been received in England from a royal palace where a crisis has arisen, no one being able to find a clockwork key or repair an automatic signal! Little trains have even been placed in harems to amuse the ladies.

The Maharajah of Gwalior had a railway that waited at table. Driven by electricity, the train would run along the table top with a load of bottles. Whenever a guest lifted his chosen drink from the wagon in which it travelled, the train remained stationary until the bottle was replaced. Locomotive, wagons and track were of solid silver.

Models also have their charm for the royal cousins Prince Chula and Prince Birabongse of Thailand. Prince Chula orders, from good makers, ship models of all kinds and particularly models of ships in which he has sailed. He once opened a model railway exhibition at Falmouth, while his cousin (we think of him as "B. Bira, the famous racing driver") used to have a model railway which could be best described as marvellous.

Taking a world-wide view, miniature railwaying is very much a royal pastime. When the Queen paid a State visit to Paris she was given a model of the Métro, the Paris Underground, for the Prince of Wales and it is more than a guess that Prince Charles' father behaved like any other father when the present arrived. At one time the railway was in his bedroom. He understands the attraction and value of models and has opened the national exhibition organized in London by *Model Engineer*, *Model Railway News* and *Model Aircraft*. This interest is not new in the Royal Family. King George VI was a model engineer who liked to slip away quietly to his lathe.

One of the earliest model locomotives was a royal present. A few weeks after the birth of the future King Edward VII in 1841 the Prince Consort ordered a number of Christmas trees to be set up as part of the celebrations at Windsor Castle. On the royal children's tree— that laden six-tiered fir which made the German Christmas tree popular in England—hung a little railway engine with a tall chimney and big driving wheels. Only eleven years had passed since the bright September morning when eight trains, the first to provide a proper passenger service by steam, pulled out of Liverpool with bands playing and thousands cheering.

Our hobby is popular, too, with rich men in business and industry. One of the American clubs, before the great financial crash of 1929, had seven millionaires among its members. After 1929 six of them were no longer millionaires—but they were still model railroaders.

When I lived in Bermuda everyone in the islands knew of the miniature track at the home of Vincent Astor. The same millionaire had another on his front lawn at Rhinebeck, New York. Despite his wealth, it was no more interesting technically than many systems built by men with ordinary incomes.

Hundreds of clergymen and doctors have their own layouts. But what of the men who work on our full-sized railways? Do they run tiny trains in their spare time or do they regard the hobby as a rather odd amusement? You would find an answer to that question in the famous railway town of Swindon, on the old Great Western. Swindon makes trains. Swindon lives by trains, Swindon *is* trains, morning, noon and all night long. And the leaders of the local model railway club are mostly West Region railway workers.

Princes, parsons and porters, medical men and millionaires, sultans, signalmen and schoolboys—every type of person is represented in the world-wide brotherhood of railway modelling.

CHAPTER THREE

Going Round in Circles

HOW can we best improve our simple railway? Let us assume for the time being that we are unable to enlarge the layout immediately. A train usually comes to us as a present and we cannot expect to add more rails right away. For the time being we must make the most of what we have.

I mention rails before anything else because they decide the whole system. It is said that a railway is as good as its track, and certainly this is true of a railway in miniature. The size and shape of layout, the lengths of run, the types of operation—all are determined by the rails.

If you have just been given an ordinary railway set, you can probably construct either a circle or an oval arrangement of curves and straights. With an uncomplicated circuit of this kind our running operations are obviously limited, at any rate in variety. Most of the time the train will be chasing its own tail. The brake-rail provided with many sets will give it a rest now and then, and a reversing gear will enable it to chase its own tail in the opposite direction for a change; but its general progress will be round-and-around, like the music in the song.

We are frequently told that a non-continuous track is closer to full-scale practice and that a "U" layout is therefore much to be preferred. Now it is true that a train from Euston to Glasgow does not swing over to Edinburgh, return to London on the King's Cross route, and then cross to Euston again for another circular journey. But it is also true that a train does not go to Scotland in order to travel from Euston to King's Cross in the same street! This is what happens on the beginner's layout. In realism (or realness, as boys sometimes call it) the U is no better than the non-U unless we imagine that the two stations are separated by a mountain which has not been tunnelled through because the journey round it is so beautiful.

Nor is the running on a U route, or any short point-to-point layout, of much interest so long as the train has only one track. Without a turntable, the beginner must either make the return journey in reverse or remove and replace the engine. He must do this frequently, for a large part of his little track, one of the curved ends of the oval, is now out of service. Extra straight rails will make the route more interesting, but it will still be less attractive than a continuous journey while the layout remains elementary.

If the rails have a bank on them—a sideways slope, with the sleeper a bit higher at one end than the other—they must be fitted together so that the slant (the super-elevation) is all the same way. It can be disappointing at first to find that the possibilities of new track arrangements are fewer than we had supposed. But we must accept these limitations happily. Above all, we must not bend a length of ordinary inflexible track or make it do what it is not intended to do.

The very young enthusiast may be forgiven his little tricks—the railway which climbs from the carpet to the top of the encyclopaedia, through a tent-like tunnel formed by opening last year's favourite annual in the middle, and on to a cereal-box station or a buffer stop closely resembling one of father's ash-trays. His idea is simply to make the train run in any way that amuses him. He just wants to play. But the older boy, the serious enthusiast, looks beyond the present moment. He hopes that his railway will grow, and so he begins at a point where growth is possible. The Slap-Happy Railway can never be improved however much we add to it, whereas the smallest and plainest layout, properly used with a sense of direction, can lead us steadily forward until a pleasure of boyhood becomes the hobby of a lifetime.

In this difference between the casual and the planned—between "Any old thing will do" and "This is the right method"—lies the whole distinction between a toy railway and a model one. Try to define the distinction in any other way and you will end in a muddle. The dividing line between models and toys can be felt better than it can be described. I am amused when the older model railwaymen and model railway writers indignantly defend themselves from any suggestion of playing trains. Some of them are even angry if a newspaper publishes a picture of schoolboys at a model railway exhibition: boys suggest toys! They regard reporters with suspicion—who knows what a reporter may not write?—and the Post Office with deep unfriendliness because it refuses to place models and toys into separate classes of mail.

All this was understandable years ago when the boy's railway was completely unlike the man's, and when the public, having little knowledge of models, lumped them together as toys, with astonishment that grown men should be interested in such things. Since then the circumstances have changed. The boy's train is as much of a model as the man's, and often of the same type; and the public in general knows what a model is. Adult men of to-day are younger in spirit than their fathers and grandfathers. If they sometimes confuse a model with a toy, they are not, as we say, looking down their noses at it. They understand that some of the loveliest and cleverest things ever to be made are toys, that a toy may be the priceless possession of a king, that toy-making is an ancient and honourable art, and that a history of toys may be a work of serious scholarship. The error now is rather on the side of the modeller in protesting too much. A brilliant mathematician, moving in a country of thought where none of us could follow him for a single step, does not object to the word *mathematics* because it includes the multiplication tables taught in an infants' school, though he might be a trifle surprised to hear someone speak of him as "doing sums"! Our wisest course, then, is to allow the word *toys* a wide meaning (like *mathematics*) so that it covers a great many things, models among them, while still drawing a line between scale models and simple toys (as between higher mathematics and Third Form decimals).

I hope that this explanation will set us right. Certainly we shall not have much success if we confine ourselves to the old argument that a model was an exact or careful copy of a larger object while a toy was merely a rough likeness. You know those tiny things stuck into cereal boxes? They are called models, and some of them deserve the name if we apply the old test of faithful representation. But on the whole they are used as toys by small children. On the other hand, the Meccano-Hornby Dinky Toys are excellent models and are widely used on seriously constructed model railways. The difference here is in the use, and so it is with your railway system.

You must not be troubled by the impossibility of keeping in line with full-scale practice. By insisting on the importance of scale and realism at every point, the old-timers tend to lead us into another muddle. One of them, a friend whom I greatly respect, told me that although a certain locomotive was a beautiful piece of

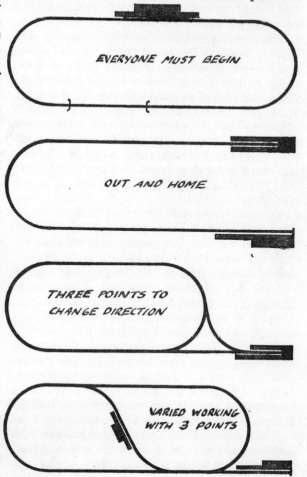

work he could not accept it as a model because it had one serious flaw: the wheel-flanges were not of correct scale size. But if we are to worry about the wheel-flanges, which are not always visible anyway, what else might we not worry about? This particular engine, for example, was supposed from its appearance to be driven by steam and was in fact driven by electricity. Surely this is a much more serious objection if we are going to object at all?

I have yet to see a full-sized steam locomotive powered by an electric motor. For that matter, there are various other aspects of miniature working, all unavoidable, which could not possibly exist at full size. The writer who solemnly insists on real procedure, who says "I know that you would like to do this, but you mustn't." has to contradict himself time and again. One evening, after making an ordinary tunnel for a very plain table layout, I sadly remarked that a real railway would not have a tunnel built like a long shed on the surface. "Don't let it worry you," said my wife. "A real railway doesn't run on a table either."

The stricter enthusiasts dislike continuous layouts, but it is far better to have a continuous track which is interesting than a point-to-point track which is respectable in the eyes of the solemn, and dull to everyone else. To quote the Reverend Edward Beal: "Some people greatly object to the idea of incorporating a *continuous run* in a layout on the ground that this is not in strict accordance with real procedure. But on the other hand it is good to remember that in real procedure a railway is never laid in a room or garage ..."

To represent a mile of actual track we would need 120 ft. of rails in O gauge, about 70 in OO and 44 in TT, the very small scale; while a truly realistic curve in TT would have to be 26 ft. in radius instead of 2 ft. We might also ask the stickler for absolute accuracy if his model expresses are about four yards long!

Even if we could overcome these limiting conditions, we should still be left with the dicffiulty of the unrealistic human factor. A giant must always be in control, and our passengers and staff are bound to be unsatisfactory unless we can kidnap some baby pixies in Cornwall or some dwarf leprechauns in Ireland. Keeping these limitations in mind, we work sensibly within them. They are not an excuse for avoiding any sort of plan or for not bothering about realism where it is possible.

We are well advised, I think, to take a tip from the artists. In the Victorian Age a painting was commonly expected to be an exact representation of something: the ideal was broadly that of the artist in ancient times who painted an apple so accurately that birds came to peck at it. But for many years past a painting has been seen as a thing in itself, an arrangement in form and colour rather than a kind of coloured photograph. The work of boys and girls in public exhibitions is normally judged in this way—not for accuracy so much as for imagination, use of colour, and balance of composition.

Similarly, a miniature railway can best be regarded as an impression: an impression which vividly suggests the real thing. I sometimes think that the boy who has a simple, busy layout, with constant movement on it, is more of a model railwayman than the adult who, in his concern to be photographic, sends a train along a straight track and then rubs his chin for a quarter of an hour, like a man playing chess. This may give pleasure to himself but is seldom of much interest to the average bystander. As beginners, we are equally entitled to build and operate our railway for pleasure, though our methods, partly from choice and partly from necessity, will be completely different. We shall hope, too, that our layout will interest others, our family and friends.

It is a mistake to move too fast. We must be content with doing a little at a time. When we have a pretty big plan in mind we naturally want to go ahead and finish it as quickly as possible, but to work for hours on end is not good for the railway or for ourselves. In particular it is not good for our tempers. We run into difficulty and out of patience.

The boy who has struggled for an afternoon or evening on a project that refuses to be a success may feel angry with himself and then with the railway. He falls into a sulky or peevish mood—which is not the best way of showing that he appreciates his model railway and would be glad of more parts for it! What he should try to do, of course, is exactly the opposite. By concentrating upon a little at a time; by not trying his patience; by not allowing his hobby to interfere with his homework, general studies or other duties; by keeping cheerful and inviting the interested attention of the family: by this behaviour he will prove that he is a true model railwayman and deserving of being helped and encouraged.

CHAPTER FOUR

Watch Those Curves

THE model railway beginner needs to be a hoarder, a miser in little things. Cardboard boxes, cigarette packets, tubular salt and pepper cartons, bits of wood and wire, illustrated catalogues and circulars, stray curtain fittings and tent-eyelets, spent matches, beads, camera spools, broken toys: the model railwayman's treasures are the unconsidered trifles which most people throw away.

One of our first actions, then, is to provide ourselves with a junk-box—or shall we call it our Materials Container? Having rescued something suitable from the dustbin, we make an arrangement with the family so that smaller things may be saved from time to time and put into the container for future use. We never know what we may need. On the other hand we must not save too much, and particularly not too much of the same stuff. Once we have a reasonable stock of cardboard and wood, we can look out for the unusual scraps—such as metal eyelets for making round windows—and ignore those which will certainly come our way again.

Matchboxes and cigarette packets offer a useful base-structure for a station. By making stations, tunnels, locomotive sheds and signal cabins we can improve the actual system enormously. A single station, however crude, will give our railway an air of purpose; place it beside a brake rail and our train has a definite point of departure and arrival. I therefore recommend that a station be our first item.

Opposite it on our circle or oval we will have another station or a tunnel. There is little more that we can do on the line itself, unless we care to add a footbridge. Instead of overcrowding the layout we turn to the area around it and see what we can do towards conjuring up a varied countryside from the perfectly level (and perfectly dull) expanse of wood. There is no reason

why this part of our work should not look pleasantly natural, for we are largely free now of the limitations imposed by the simplicity of our track. While our station and tunnel have to be elementary, the landscape can be planned and developed much more fully.

If you are likely to install a smaller gauge in the future—if you expect, let us say, to change from gauge O clockwork to gauge OO electric—you may argue that the work you are doing at present will then be out of scale. While this is true, you should not be discouraged by it. At least some of the groundwork will be suitable for your new layout, while the ideas and skill which you have gained are bound to be a great help. If you are sure of making the change before long, you may even prefer to design your landscape accordingly, so that you are running one railway and planning another. In any event, no one will be shocked if your buildings and other details are too large at this stage. The average beginner makes them too large anyway.

There is little point in providing the newcomer with actual designs. Everything depends on his particular circumstances. A visit to a well-stocked model shop or handicraft dealer's will give him plenty of suggestions for a new project. Almost every imaginable kind of constructional aid may be obtained from these two sources. Building papers, for example are sold in more than thirty varieties. Do you want red brick or smoky brick? Is there anything you can do with an archway? Just a glance at these sheets is inspiration enough.

I strongly urge you to see what you can buy in the way of modelling materials before you begin to construct anything yourself. The average book on model railway construction is intended for the modeller with a good deal of skill and a great amount of patience. It assumes that he would prefer to make even those parts which can be bought quite cheaply. The author is probably an expert, and when he tells us that a certain process is simple he is thinking in terms of his own skill rather than of ours. Most of his schemes we are unable to attempt, and the rest are not worth our attempting when so much first-class constructional material can be had from the model shop. It is the little aids which are most useful—the roof-ridges, the Bovril posters, the destination plates and the numerous other things that add greatly to the appearance of our railway and are all the more effective because of their professional touch. So far as detail work is concerned, the beginner will get more useful ideas from catalogues and advertisements than from construction books. To make the main body of a building from odds-and-ends is fairly easy. The difficulty lies in the next stage, when the raw work has to be transformed into a finished article; and it is here that the manufactured items are a boon.

As soon as we have carried out our first plans and have at least a station, we may consider enlarging our railway. What a difference the extra rails will make! Our eagerness to buy track, to spend all our pocket-money on it for a while, will lead us into getting the wrong things unless we know just what we want to do. There are several types of track, apart from the further distinction between two-rail and three-rail. We can get the conventional type as supplied with the train sets, the type which is sold in kit form for assembly at home, and the flexible type which can be curved, straightened, and curved again. The kit tracks and the flexible ones are realistic, strong and reasonably priced. They can be fitted to conventional tinplate track, providing of course that the gauge is the same.

Which kind shall we choose? Most of us with ordinary ready-made track will continue with it. If we turn to another kind we shall do so because we are changing the whole type of layout. Non-flexible ready-made track remains popular. It has the advantage of being familiar and the virtue of being generally convenient for the average boy. It is certainly the safest choice for the beginner.

As far as possible we should keep to the same kind throughout. A device may now be had for linking ordinary track to scale track, but this does not make a mixture of tracks any more desirable. The choice in the first place is often not our own, the rails having come with the rest of the set as a present. But if we much prefer a different type in the same gauge, and if we intend to introduce it eventually, we should not let the layout expand before we change over. When our railway is much bigger our present layout will be only a part of it, and we can then use the old rails rather cunningly in tunnels and other places where they will not be seen or immediately noticed. As it is impossible, except with a very big layout, to hide a large number of rails in this way, our new track should be introduced pretty soon if we intend to change at all. A uniform track not only looks better; it gives better running as well.

The temptation is strong to buy curves. They seem to us more interesting than straight rails, besides being of great importance when our working area is small and the line must keep doubling back. The use of curves for their own sake is a common error—and a bad one too, for it leads to weirdly complicated layouts and difficult running, whereas a few straights will enlarge the whole system surprisingly, help to keep the general design realistic, and produce continuously smooth running that is a pleasure to watch.

By careful planning we can make sure of getting the curves which we clearly need instead of building up a random collection. The planning is essential. We must know exactly what we want to do and what space we have for doing it. Curves require more room that we often expect, and we may also need more of them for a particular purpose than we had supposed. The manufacturers supply us with comparatively large circles made up of a good many separate lengths, and so we have to beware of building a curved section which is too big and, on the other hand, of misjudging the number of separate curved pieces which the section requires. If we are apt to get too many curves, we are still more liable to find ourselves a curve short when we come to make up a plan. How many beginners, I wonder, have fallen into this simple and annoying error!

As we nearly always begin with enough track to form a circle, we should keep in mind the number of lengths that the circle contains. A Hornby-Dublo three-rail circle of $17\frac{1}{4}$ in. radius (2 ft. $10\frac{1}{2}$ in. diameter) is formed of eight curved pieces; a two-rail Hornby-Dublo circle of $17\frac{1}{4}$ in. radius requires twelve. Shorter curved lengths may be obtained.

RADII						
	2 or 3 rail	Standard Curve	Half Curve	Quarter Curve	Large Radius Curve	Curves in Circle
Hornby Dublo	3 rail	15″	15″	15″	17¼″	8
	2 rail	15″	15″	15″	17¼″	12
Tri-ang	2 rail Standard	13½″	13½″	—	17⅛″	12
	2 rail Series 3	13½″	13½″	—	17⅛″	12
Tri-ang TT	2 rail Type A	10⁹⁄₁₆″	12″	—	12″	8
	2 rail Type B	10⁹⁄₁₆″	12″	—	12″	8
Trix	3 rail	13½″	13½″	13½″	15¾″*	12
Rivarossi	2 rail	40 cm.	—	—	—	12
	—	—	—	—	60 cm.*	18
Lionel HO	3 rail	15″	15″	—	18″*	12
Märklin	3 rail centre stud contact	15″	15″	15″	—	12
		12″	—	—	—	8
		—	—	—	16″*	12

* These large radii curves are obtainable in more than one length.

Tri-ang similarly offers a choice of curves. One circle is 17⅛ in., very close to the large radius in Hornby-Dublo, and the other is 13½ in., not so close. The choice applies to both kinds of Tri-ang track, the familiar Standard track, with raised plastic base, and the Tri-ang Series 3 which has open-spaced sleepers and can be connected to the Standard by a simple clip device known as a track underlay. Whichever size of circle and whichever kind of track we prefer, the number of lengths that we need is twelve.

The modern Trix system is a big improvement on the old arrangement, for alternating current trains, of three hollow tinplate rails on a bakelite base. In the Trix direct current system, hollow tinplate running-rails rest on cut-out imitation-fibre sleepers, and there is a third centre-rail of special type, very much like its counterpart in actual practice. The curves are no longer all to a radius of 13½ in. With the introduction of 15¾ in. radius, we now have "curved small" and "curved large". Besides stating the radius and length in inches, Trix gives the curvature of the rails in degrees, so that the complete description may read: "Curved large radius 2, 30 degrees, 8¾ in., 15¾ in. radius." Railway surveyors and engin-

eers obtain the figure in degrees by dividing the radius in feet by 114.54, the number of degrees in a radian; thus a curve of ten degrees is of 1,145 ft. radius. But this leads us into geometry and we shall be content to speak of large and small radius without bothering about the degree of curvature.

The curves on a model railway are much sharper than those in real practice. Our high-speed traffic requires a radius of about a mile, and a radius of 1,320 ft.—twenty chains, as a surveyor would say—is considered dangerous enough for special precautions to be taken. When we know that a 2 ft. curve on an O gauge layout represents a curve of only 87 ft. at full scale, we realize that our model locomotives are continually travelling on bends that would be impossible on a real railway. As it is, certain adjustments have to be made in the designs of miniature engines and rolling stock. Wheels on the leading bogies of a locomotive (a bogie is really a little swivelling truck underneath the engine) are smaller than true scale-size when their side-swing, if they were of correct size, would throw them against the outside cylinders. Because of the swing, too, long vehicles must be freely coupled. If a curve is too sharp the buffers at the front of a coach or truck may catch in those at the rear of the vehicle immediately ahead. This buffer-locking and the derailment of tank engines (especially 0-4-4 tanks) are well-known troubles on beginners' layouts, while the more advanced model railwayman occasionally has an accident with a couple of corridor coaches when the special connection between then is not free enough for a sharp curve.

You will see that the model railway and the real railway have the same need for gradual curves wherever they can be used. The running is freer and safer when the swing is not abrupt. If we are puzzled by frequent derailments at a particular point on our layout, the cause may well be a sudden swing from a straight run to a curve which is too small in radius. We must try to avoid these sudden swings—above all the double swing created by a reverse or S curve. The beginner who likes a fancy (or crazy) touch on his line will constantly come to grief here.

In understanding the advantages of larger curves we must not forget, as we so easily can, the space that a curve occupies. Main-line curves may enlarge the general layout more than we had bargained for, with the result that we have to alter either the baseboard or the whole

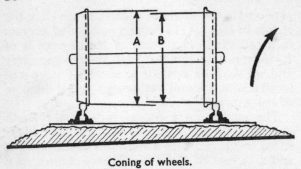

Coning of wheels.

design. While planning will prevent this diffi-culty, the construction of sidings when we arrive at that stage will give us a few problems. Sidings come within our overall framework, and we do not know at the beginning what we shall want to do later when we can give more attention to shunting and have more rolling stock to be accommodated off the main line. Our difficulty with sidings will come from the need of small curves for reasons of space, with the awkward-ness of shunting on sharp turns where buffer-locking is a nuisance.

Small curves increase the load for the engine. What the engine wants is to go smoothly ahead on the straight. The curve of a rail forces a change of direction, and the resistance adds to the load. We soon discover that a locomotive does its best hauling on a straight run.

Everyone has noticed that the tread of an engine wheel, the part that rests on the rail top, has a slope on it. If I may be excused for mentioning geometry once more, the tread is in effect the bottom slice of a cone with the flange at the base. A piece of paper placed around the tread so that it exactly followed the slope would look like a tiny dunce's cap. Consequently we speak of the treads as being coned.

They are not coned just for fun. Yet very few model railwaymen give this detail a second thought, and very few of the second thoughts are correct. The slope is not simply to keep the flanges safely on the inner side of the rails. It has the more complicated purpose of acting like the differential gear on a motor car. When a four-wheeled vehicle travels in a curve, the outer and inner wheels are moving along different arcs. Looking at their tyre marks on a muddy surface we should see that one arc was smaller

than the other. Thus the outside wheels have to go farther; and to go farther in the same time they must go faster if the vehicle is to make the bend naturally, without skidding. No difficulty at all exists when each wheel is free to turn at its own speed, as on a stationary axle. But when each wheel is driven from the same source, when each is fixed to a moving axle instead of being loose on a fixed one, a way must be found of providing for the two different speeds. The differential gear which makes this adjustment for the back wheels of a motor car would not be practicable on a railway engine. Instead we have the coned tread.

An engine taking a curve wants, as I have mentioned, to continue along the straight—to travel on a tangent to the curve—and so the outer wheels press hard against the outer rail. Having failed to defy the curve, it then obeys the order given to it by the rails. But the outward swing is still there. If you whirl a pail of water round and round, the pail will want to fly away from you—and so will the water, which is why it remains in the pail. The same centrifugal force keeps our engine swinging outwards. All the way, the flanges on the outside wheels rub against the rail. This means that the outer wheels are running on the part of the tread near-est to the flange—the bottom part of the cone. Hence the engine is, in effect, provided with slightly larger outside wheels for the bend, while the inside wheels have become slightly smaller in the sense that they are running on the narrower, outer end of the sloping tread. The gauge on curved rails is adjusted to allow more side play, so that the wheels can swing into these positions.

Now, I have explained the coning of wheel-treads at some length not because it is enor-mously important, but because it is interesting. It is interesting for its own sake and also as an example of the thought and care that have been spent on designing a miniature railway engine. I think that we might tell the family about coning, especially if they are inclined to sniff at "playing with trains". As for ourselves, we shall try to use something of the same thought and care when we move on to the more varied and exciting layouts which become possible with the use of points.

Above : Paddington ahead, Birkenhead behind. "King Edward VII" drawing the 8.5 a.m.

Below : At York, on down train from Newcastle : 4-6-2 "Happy Knight."

ATCHISON, TOPEKA AND SANTA FE

All the romance of railways is found in the story of the Santa Fe. In the 1880's (*left*) the track pushes west from Alburquerque. (*Right*) The roundhouse at Nickerson, Kansas, in 1886.

(*Left*) Topeka in 1880 when the railway had been fighting the Denver and Rio Grande for a canyon pass 2,000 ft. high and 10 yds. wide. (*Right*) The Chicagoan pulls into modern Topeka.

The High Level El Capitan (*left*) climbs to the crest of Raton Pass. (*Right*) The diesel sheds at Argentine are neat and trim—but who can resist a steam giant like the one below?

(*Santa Fe pictures*)

Hornby No. 40 Tank and goods brake van.

Grace in every line of Tri-ang's "Princess Royal".

A sturdy clockwork saddletank by Tri-ang.

The Hornby-Dublo "Bristol Castle".

The L.N.E.R. inspired the Hornby N2.

A realistic Tri-ang steeplecab; the pantograph is not used.

Railwaymen admire this Tri-ang dock shunter.

. . . and the Real Thing

Class C.14 in service at Eastleigh on B.R. Southern Region.
(*L. Elsey*)

Saddletank No. 17 at Greenwich Gas Works. (*Brian Western*)

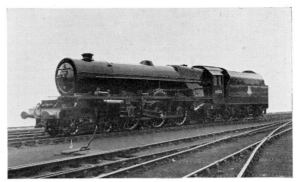

N46203 "Princess Margaret Rose" on B.R. Midland Region.
(*British Railways*)

N7 Class 0-6-2T of B.R. Eastern Region at Stratford, London.
(*Oliver Smith*)

No. 5017 "The Gloucester Regiment", a Castle Class locomotive on B.R. Western Region. (*British Railways*)

Bagnall 0-6-0 208 h.p. locomotive, as supplied to the National Coal Board. (*W. G. Bagnall Ltd.*)

Swiss steeplecab shunting locomotive.
(*Swiss National Railways*)

A study in harmony between Marseilles and Nice.   (French Railways)

Here, too, the train blends with the background—forests in Germany.   (German State Railways)

CC7107 flies over a level crossing on the run that broke all records (205 m.p.h.)   *(French Railways)*

Only an aircraft could keep pace with BB9004 at speed. The pilot's view.   *(French Railways)*

The twentieth century in an ancient land.

Canadian Pacific diesel freight train in the famous Spiral Tunnels of the Rockies.

No fancy portal here; straight into the heart of Mount Othello, British Columbia.

(Canadian Pacific Railway)

CHAPTER FIVE

Away We Go

POINTS make all the difference. As soon as we get our first pair, we enter a new and greater stage in our progress. Right away we escape from the limitations of a single route: we can have a sidings or branch line with all the variety in working that is offered by a more complicated layout. Our whole railway is changed by a single item. No other item will ever change it so much.

The snag is cost. Compared with plain track, points are expensive. It is hard to postpone buying as many as eight ordinary straight pieces or curves in order to get one piece which adds little to the running length. Nevertheless we should introduce a pair of points as soon as possible. Points are well worth the temporary sacrifice of other track, for their effect is to extend the railway far more than mere length can extend it. Our simple layout may be made bigger by adding straights and curves, but it will remain simple until we are able to send our engine from one line on to another. The only way of doing this is by points.

On the actual railway the points assembly, the special rail for changing the direction of a vehicle, is known as a lead or turnout. It consists of a pair of switches with closure and check rails, a crossing (referred to as common or acute, according to the sharpness of the angle) and various other parts. The points, to a railwayman, are not the whole arrangement but the switches themselves, which is what we should expect, for the switches or moving rails are narrow at the ends so that they fit against the main rails (the stock rails) and lead the train— trick it, in a sense—on to its new course. Both *points* and *lead* are straightforward words. The term *crossing*, too, explains itself and is less mysterious than *frog*, a term used by modellers everywhere, and by railwaymen in America, but

not by those who work on the permanent way in Britain. Talk about frogs to a platelayer on British Railways, and he will think either that your conversation is rather odd or that your eyesight is better than his!

Strictly speaking, it is incorrect to speak of *point sleepers*. To a railwayman a sleeper—in America a *tie* or *cross-tie*, which is completely sensible—means the beam used with plain track. Sleepers for points and crossing work are *timbers*. As a sleeper is normally 8 ft. 6 in. long, 10 in. wide and 5 in. thick, and a crossing timber 12 in. wide, 6 in. thick and of the special length required, the use of two different terms is readily understood.

Every occupation has its own jargon or lingo, but our need is to communicate, and those of us who are not railwaymen may well prefer to employ words whose meaning is clear to most other people. Expert model railwaymen frequently speak of a *turnout*, which is correct, but in their zeal for accuracy they somehow imagine that the word *points*, as used by the ignorant public, is wrong. They insist on *point* and are wrong themselves. The correct term is *points* with *pair of points* as the alternative.

Now that we are clear on these points—if you will forgive me—we may consider the new opportunities that open before us when our track is no longer an elementary circuit. We shall begin with either a right-hand or a left-hand turnout. Planning tells us which we need. Although the difference between the two is extremely simple, mistakes often occur because the beginner, looking at a drawing of his layout, sees the assembly the wrong way round. The best way of keeping the correct picture in one's mind is to imagine that one is travelling along the straight part of the assembly and intending to swing off on to the curved part. With a

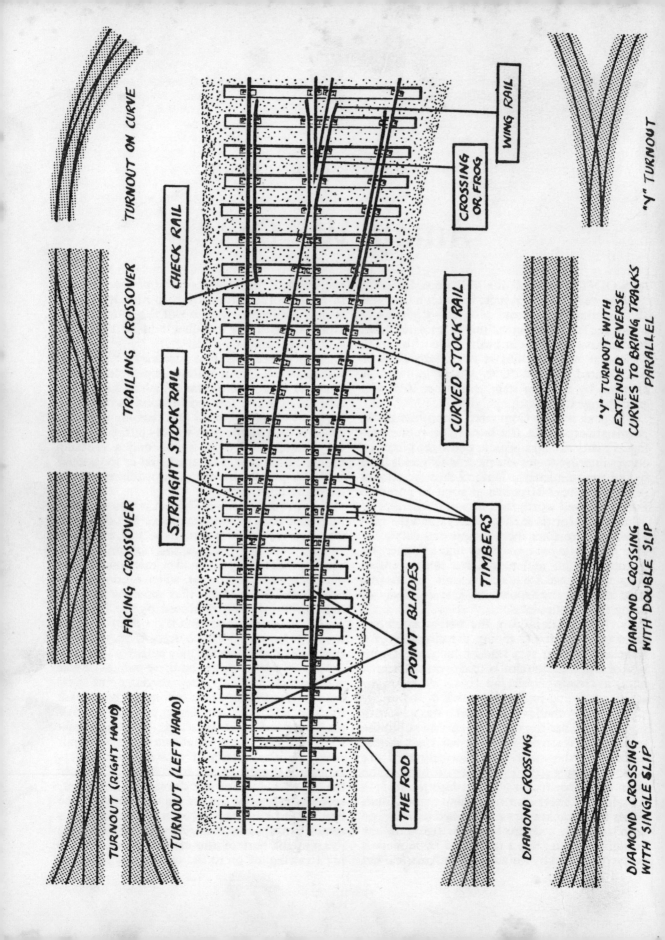

TURNOUT ON CURVE

WING RAIL

CROSSING OR FROG

"Y" TURNOUT

CHECK RAIL

TRAILING CROSSOVER

CURVED STOCK RAIL

"Y" TURNOUT WITH EXTENDED REVERSE CURVES TO BRING TRACKS PARALLEL

STRAIGHT STOCK RAIL

FACING CROSSOVER

TIMBERS

POINT BLADES

DIAMOND CROSSING WITH DOUBLE SLIP

TURNOUT (RIGHT HAND)

TURNOUT (LEFT HAND)

THE ROD

DIAMOND CROSSING

DIAMOND CROSSING WITH SINGLE SLIP

right-hand turnout the curve is to one's right.

When we picture ourselves travelling along the straight, only one direction will enable us to use the points at all. We have to run right into the curve, and so we must be going towards it—going in the direction that it will swing us away. If we switch to the right on a clockwise route we are not able to switch to the right at the same spot when we run anti-clockwise, from right to left, for the curve is then away from us, pointing back. The points are *facing* when we can use them on our journey without reversing and *trailing* when they are in the opposite direction.

With a single left-hand or right-hand turnout and a short length of plain rail we can at once provide our first sidings. It is advisable at this stage to have a buffer-stop. We may be able to make our own, perhaps from a small wooden block and a piece of broken track which can be twisted into the familiar shape. The difficulty is not so much in the construction as in the fitting afterwards. A buffer-stop looks a bit silly if a train bumps it away every time. On the other hand, it should not be a big cumbrous thing. A rough-and-ready buffer-stop gives a crude look to the whole railway, while a neat one has exactly the opposite effect. For this reason, I would recommend a couple of stops at a very early stage to improve the simplest point-to-point line.

A buffer-stop is far from being a luxury. In addition to enhancing the appearance of the layout, it serves an important practical purpose. While many of the items on a table railway, from water-towers to slot machines, cannot be used like the originals which they represent, a model buffer-stop performs precisely the same duty as a real one: it provides a terminal. Every point-to-point track should be closed at the ends. When I was very small I had a clockwork locomotive which ran off the edge of a table and never ran again—a disaster that is by no means rare.

The ready-made buffer-stop has a neat, sturdy appearance. We can get the ordinary kind or the hydraulic. In actual practice the hydraulic system uses oil as a cushion for the oncoming engine, the two buffer-heads being on long shafts or rods which are mounted in cylinders so that the impact of the engine buffers forces them back against the pressure of the oil inside. We can use this type for our main-line terminal and the other type for our sidings. If we build our own we can always end a short

line with a plain beam at buffer height, but the structure looks more businesslike when there are buffer-heads on the beam. I am thinking purely of appearance; a main line at a big station may end in a very simple structure.

We shall not be hanged, drawn and quartered if, like most people, we refer to a station buffer-stop as "the buffers". For all that, it would be sensible of us to agree at the beginning on the words we shall use (without too much fussiness) if only for the practical reason that their use makes it easier to distinguish between one thing and another. The buffers are on the vehicle; the buffer-stop, with or without buffer-heads, is at the terminal.

Now, a buffer-stop should not be regarded as a barrier to be crashed into; it is much more like the full-stop at the end of a sentence. We shall no doubt have some alarming trips at first. Despite their entertainment value, they must not be allowed to continue once we have the means of preventing them. A violent bump every so often may harm the engine and will certainly do it no good. Nor are we running a true model railway if we encourage violent stops or do nothing to prevent them. At full-scale our line would be notorious.

With a clockwork locomotive the power can be adjusted to the length of the run. We hold a series of trials, beginning with a light winding and then increasing the number of turns until we know just how many are needed for a particular journey. To gauge the engine power in this way is one of the greatest pleasures of clockwork railwaying. It gives satisfaction to ourselves and to any who may be looking. Whenever a spring runs down in the course of a journey we realize, sometimes with annoyance, the chief drawback of clockwork. Not to have this happen is a tremendous help. With a cosy feeling of being in control, we see our train come to a standstill at the intended point.

Planned winding does not displace the advantages to be gained from fitting a brake-rail. For track-braking to be possible, the engine must have a suitable lever underneath it. The engine is halted by turning another lever at the track-side so that a metal arm or ramp rises between the rails and snaps on the brake. In track-reversing a similar device causes the wheels to revolve the other way when a reversing lever is struck.

This system allows the clockwork locomotive to be controlled on its actual journey as it can-

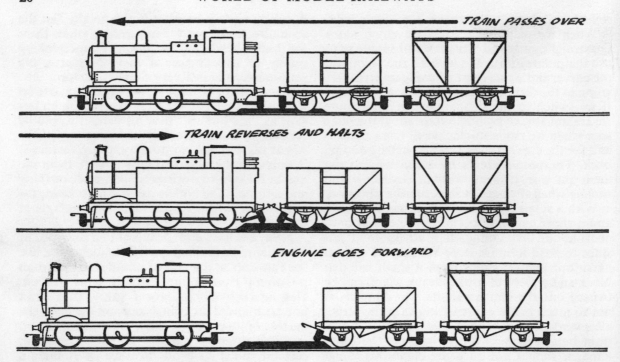

not be from the cab. Its value is so great that the beginner should consult the catalogues and acquaint himself with the types of special rail for his own layout whether he uses clockwork or electricity. To leave the benefits of track-control until later is a big mistake. An uncoupling rail, for example, is an immense asset to the smallest and plainest circuit because it provides a delightfully neat and automatic means of varying the make-up of the train. Some of our arrangements will probably be rather odd, but they will none the less keep our interest refreshed. We shall be eager to add another rail—and it is then that we may regret our failure to appreciate the value of track-control a little earlier.

To the newcomer an excess of track seems an impossibility. Dreaming of a larger and larger layout, he gives little or no thought to the question of where he will put it. Only when he comes to lay a branch line or a siding does he suddenly discover that his house is not quite the size of the Albert Hall! Not infrequently at this stage he already has too much ordinary track; or will have too much when he adds the special units that should have been incorporated before his railway began to grow.

It is because an extension line emphasizes the value of control from the track that I have left the discussion of this subject until now. As soon

as we introduce points, certain other features take on a new importance. On our elementary circuit two or three control rails were a boon that we much enjoyed: on our sidings or branch line they are a necessity if we intend our operations to be efficient and natural-looking.

The types of control are decided by the circumstances. A brake-rail or reversing rail would be useless with an electric engine or with a clockwork engine not designed for it. Nor is anything achieved by installing an uncoupling rail unless the couplings on the train are automatic. We may care to note that Tri-ang couplings are the same in both clockwork and electric, that the track is also the same, and that the only essential difference between the two systems lies in the motive power. Since January 1959 Mk. 3 couplings have been a standard fitting on all Tri-ang OO/HO locomotives and rolling stock. They will operate with the old Mk. 2 couplings, and the Series Three uncoupling track may be used with either. Tri-ang, Trix and Hornby all employ the principle of the raised ramp between the running rails. On a Tri-ang layout the couplings are released by bringing the train to a halt above the raised ramp and then reversing the engine a little. When the train is travelling normally the couplings are not affected by the ramp as the pull of the engine keeps them taut. Their special design makes them unsuitable for rolling stock of other makes.

Having begun with the products of one company, we must not add those of another unless we are certain that the two kinds are on speaking terms. Although we know that the change-over is better avoided, we may be tempted now and again to add an odd item simply because it attracts us or has come our way more or less by accident, as in the offer of an exchange. We should be aware of these opportunities, and never more than when the item is an article of rolling stock. The proud coaches of one company may not want to know the proud coaches of another even when they have been introduced. All locomotives and rolling stock in Hornby-Dublo and Trix are equipped with couplings of the Peco type (a Pritchard Patent) and will operate only with vehicles whose couplings are of this design. Among the Continental makes familiar in Britain, the vehicles manufactured by Märklin, which is German, may be hitched to those in the Rivarossi system, which is Italian, but not to others; while the tiny Liliput vehicles, of Austrian origin, will connect with rolling stock by Rivarossi, Pocher, and Hag. and Kleinbahn.

It is a mistake to assume that because two vehicles can be coupled without difficulty they are bound to run easily on the same track. We must make sure first, and to do this we should conduct a thorough trial over the circuit. The boy who takes with him a length of plain straight track, carries out a test on it, and is satisfied, may have a shock when he tries to send his new piece of rolling stock over a pair of points.

A vehicle will travel properly at a turnout or crossing only if it has the appropriate back-to-back measurement. This sounds highly technical and mysterious but is seen to be quite simple when we consider what happens at the places where one track meets another. Let us study a points assembly for a moment. The first thing we notice, if we have never studied one before, is that two of the long rails have stopped short and two very short ones have sprung up from nowhere. There are breaks and gaps, and the reason for them is clear as soon as we let our eye travel along, like the engine, from one track to another. Without breaks a train could not turn off or go straight on, as we desire. The space must be small enough for each wheel to travel across it when the train switches off from the straight, and big enough for each wheel to pass through when the train is not changing direction.

Here we have to reckon with the swing of the wheels. So narrow is the gap that the normal swing has to be checked or the flanges would not pass. Consequently we have short pieces of rail parallel with the main rail to keep the flanges a little to that side. Caught between the long rail and the short one, the wheels are guided on the right course.

Opposite each check-rail is a somewhat similar piece, the wing-rail. Instead of being chopped off abruptly, one of the curved rails ends in a straight bit which forms the inner side of a channel. Thus both the left-hand and right-hand wheels have to pass along a narrow space between parallel rails. The space exactly fits the design of rolling stock which is intended to use the track, and so any other make that travels on it must also fit exactly. It must have the same back-to-back measurement, which means the distance between the backs of a pair of wheels on an axle measured at the level of the flange.

This explanation, like so much else which looks complicated, is not at all difficult if we take it step by step, with the help of a diagram or of an actual turnout. In the course of following it, we have learnt a good deal more about these fascinating points which make all the difference to our railway.

CHAPTER SIX

"There is Your Railway!"

WHEN you are in a train, do you ever marvel at the amount of work that went to the making of the railways? Hills had to be cut through or flattened, valleys and rivers to be bridged, dips to be filled, and everything to be cleared from the path. If the human race perished and all our buildings, books and pictures were destroyed, there would still be great holes through great mountains to puzzle and impress any visitors from outer space who explored our lonely planet, even a thousand years afterwards.

Just before the Canadian Pacific line was completed through the Rockies, the Governor-General of Canada ordered a silver spike to be made. But the engineers felt that it would be more fitting to use a spike of iron. "I suppose," said Dugald McKenzie, who piloted the work train in carrying the last sleepers and rails, "they think we had caviare for lunch and breakfast served us in bed". The task of building the 3,000-mile railway had been prodigious.

If we are awed by the grandeur of the Rockies, we are amazed and thrilled by the railway that crosses them on the run from the prairies to the Pacific. At Kicking Horse Pass the track spirals up inside the solid mountain. In some places, bridges hang like spiders' webs in the air; at other points, the line seems to have been plastered against the vast walls of rock towering from thunderous rivers to the silent kingdom of the clouds.

Parts of the route cost as much as half a million dollars a mile when a dollar was worth much more than it is to-day. Towards the other end, on the north shore of Lake Superior, twelve million dollars had to be spent on two hundred miles, and of this sum more than two millions went up in smoke—the acrid smoke from dynamite. Twelve steamships brought materials and food across the water, two thousand horse-teams carried the cargoes from the lake shore, and twelve thousand men from almost every country toiled through the long day to the luxury of nightfall with a rough log-cabin supper and the songs of home.

Between these triumphs, between the marvels in the Rockies and those achieved along the shore of Lake Superior, what other wonders do we find! Sweating and cursing, laughing and singing, the rabble army led by William Cornelius Van Horne hacked and blasted its way from ocean to ocean.

All over North America the railways spelt out, in the relentless rhythm of hammer on spike, their magnificent epics of optimism justified. The Atchison, Topeka and Santa Fe was described as a "railroad that began nowhere and is going nowhere", and the description was not unfair to a line which, with one second-hand locomotive, one battered passenger coach and a dozen freight cars, had set out to push through a wilderness whose population fell short of two to the square mile.

As the men of the Union Pacific raced their rivals of the Central Pacific, Indians swooped down on them to raid and burn and kill. Troubles broke out among the men themselves, and the camp-followers in their hells-on-wheels were completely unembarrassed by the Ten Commandments. "Are the gamblers quiet and behaving?" asked General Dodge of the U.P. "You bet they are," replied General Jack S. Casement. "They're quiet and behaving out there in the graveyard!"

Through everything, the work continued at a phenomenal pace. "It is a grand Anvil Chorus," wrote an unknown journalist, "that those sturdy sledges are playing across the plains. It is in triple time, three strokes to a spike. There are ten spikes to a rail, four hundred rails to a mile, eighteen hundred miles to San Francisco."

The last spike of all, the golden spike, was driven by Governor Stanford into a sleeper of polished laurel when at last the engines of the rival lines stood head-to-head where the tracks met. Wires connected the sleeper to the telegraph system so that, at the exact moment, the whole nation might rejoice at the completion of "the greatest work ever undertaken by man". In New York, at Trinity Church, the Te Deum was sung at noon; in Philadelphia bells rang; in Omaha a hundred guns boomed; in Chicago the triumphal parade stretched for four miles. San Francisco just went crazy.

In America and Switzerland, and in every country where the scenery is on a grand scale, the railway engineers worked in the spirit of Van Horne who reported, after his survey of the Lake Superior route, that he had in front of him "two hundred miles of engineering impossibilities"—and then went ahead, accepting the impossible as a challenge. But when we consider the problems to be solved on even the least exciting routes we see that every good-sized railway is a wonder. A line across flat country, though comparatively easy to lay, needed a special road like any other, and the road was made by moving thousands of tons of soil.

The geographical difficulties, such as mountains and rivers, were not the only problems and sometimes not the worst. In England, where people had been living for hundreds of years and a good deal of the countryside was like a garden, every mile brought some special obstacle: a village or farm, a row of houses, an ancient or beautiful site which a railway would spoil, or a piece of private land which the owner wanted to keep as it was.

By no means all the opposition came from the owners of land and from canal companies with a natural dislike of the steam-engine. In many places whole communities rose in anger. The railway surveyors were met by men armed with sticks, pitchforks and guns. At Addington, after a skirmish, they were fined; at Saxby they were locked up in the county gaol. In Oxfordshire the fighting was fierce, and in districts less inclined to violence the railway men were followed about by boys and girls who shouted rude names and threw stones.

Faced with such enmity, the surveyors adopted every trick that occurred to them. They appeared suddenly, with their theodolites and white sticks, while the local people were at church. At the suggestion of George Stephenson, some of them tried to work in the moonlight—only to be discovered by the gamekeepers. On one occasion Stephenson thought of another trick. He sent off a decoy party with guns, and when the gamekeepers heard the guns fired in the moonlight they hurried to the spot, in the belief that poachers were abroad. The surveyors, who had been waiting in another place, were then free to act.

Against all opposition, the railway went forward mile by mile. Opening the door one morning, a startled householder would find a white flag planted in the garden path: the surveyors' notice that the railway was to go, like the one in the song, right through the middle of the house—which would of course be torn down first. One man was told that if he objected to having the railway near his lawn it would be taken through his kitchen instead.

The Russian way was much simpler. When the Czar Nicholas was asked to decide the route of the intended railway between St Petersburg (now Leningrad) and Moscow, he tossed the plans aside, put his sword across the map, and drew a straight line from one city to the other. "There," he said, "is your railway."

If, in planning our miniature line, we have to take more thought than the Czar of all the Russias, we also do not run into the trouble which dogged the English railway surveyors—unless we try to take over the whole dining room or drive the rest of the family into a corner! Whatever we hope to do with our layout, and whatever the size of our working-space, we must carry out a survey. I have made several brief references to planning and I am giving it greater attention now because it becomes much more important as our railway begins to extend.

As soon as we add our first pair of points we shall think seriously of our layout as we intend it to be, in broad outline. How the details will take shape we do not yet know, but we need to have a clear idea of our routes and general working. The importance of this will be obvious once we have laid our sidings or branch-line and are ready to get our second turnout. Like the surveyors and engineers, we have to know where we are going.

For most of us the determining factor is space. We realize the smallness of the average house when we want to add an article of modest

City of Truro, the first locomotive to attain a speed of 100 m.p.h.

size, such as a long-playing gramophone. With a model railway the problem is much greater because our choice of space, in so far as we have a choice, is strongly governed by the further factor of place. A long-player is a mechanical device disguised as a piece of furniture. Whatever its position in the living-room, its right to be in the room is unquestioned. But a miniature railway, besides occupying precious space, has the air of an intruder. It is not an article of furniture—at any rate when we are using it.

In our earliest days as model railwaymen we manage fairly well, apart from wearing a slightly haunted look on occasion. Having laid out our railway and operated it for a spell, we pack it up again, sometimes contentedly and sometimes with a long sad sigh that less important matters should break in upon our pleasure. To set out the track, and to take it up afterwards, is then part of the routine and is not at all difficult.

As we extend our railway and build up the area around it, we are less happy with our old procedure of moving everything separately. It is time now for the layout to be made into a permanent unit so that the parts, which are growing in number, do not have to be arranged and dismantled each time. Unless we fasten the parts to a base, we shall eventually come to the point of having to begin taking the railway to pieces as soon as we finish putting it together!

Besides saving us trouble, and reducing the wear-and-tear which affects the track and other items when they are constantly being moved, a fixed layout is in every way far more satisfying than a temporary one. What we achieve on Friday evening is still solidly there on Saturday afternoon. We do not have to fiddle, and scratch our heads, and fiddle again, just to make something exactly as it was. Our work is before us, like a picture.

We must get a baseboard. If we are keeping to our table-top, we can place the board on it and so bring our railway to the table. The size of the board will of course depend upon the size of the table-top on which it rests. It may be a little larger. In wanting to have it as big as possible, we must be careful not to have it too big or it will tilt. Wooden clamps can sometimes be fixed underneath to hold the loose sheet of wood to the firm wood of the table.

In allowing ourselves this extra space we shall be guided by the weight and sturdiness of the board. But wait: the board has to be carried about, and if we are going to move it from room to another—perhaps from a bedroom to the sitting room and up again—we had better restrain our craving for bigness unless we intend to train as furniture removers. The difficulty is overcome by having the board in sections, providing that we can also overcome the difficulty of fitting the sections neatly together. Here again a system of clamping may be used, each section being gripped firmly to the table-top.

What type of wood shall we get? To choose a piece of board merely because it looks right is to invite the risk of being landed with something totally unsuitable. As a first requirement, the board must be of a kind which will take nails and hold them properly. Hardboard is often regarded as too tough and Celotex as too soft. But both are used. One modeller will recommend Celotex and another will advise us against it. One will tell us that there is nothing to beat plywood and another will insist that plywood is bound to warp. Before we let ourselves be influenced by a judgment based on someone else's experience we should know the full circumstances. What did John Smith do with his board? Where did he keep it? Was it firm or springy?

Insulation board needs to be half an inch thick and plywood a quarter of an inch. Crosspieces are added for stiffening, according to the thickness of the board, its tendency to warp, and its size. The board should be stored in a place where the temperature is normal and the atmosphere free from damp. When rather thin sheets are used the size must be considered in relation to warping, bending and cracking, for a board which is firm enough in a piece a yard square may be unsuitable in a larger piece. With Compo board the width should not exceed four feet.

The material known as grooved-and-tongued board is excellent in a thickness of half an inch, and some of us may consider it worth the extra cost when we are buying only a small quantity. Our most sensible plan is to consult the local Do-It-Yourself merchant. In buying anything at a handicraft shop it is always wise to explain what we are intending to do. The dealer, if he is a worthy member of the trade, will then try to help us from his special and up-to-date knowledge of artificial boards and other materials. My own dealer, heedless of his Saturday afternoon queue, will spend five minutes explaining how I can do something an easier way and save threepence to boot.

For a first-class baseboard I recommend the use of two sheets, one of them serving as an overlay. A sheet of Celotex or beaverboard stuck over a sheet of plywood or slightly heavier Plyscore will reduce running-noises. The method may be used with various materials, some of which would not be highly satisfactory in a single sheet. Consequently the beginner who is not happy with his baseboard may have bought wisely after all, so long as he adds a second layer.

Sound-proofing is not the trivial luxury that it may seem. A plain baseboard acts as a sounding-board—very effectively indeed when the legs supporting it are far apart. As a single locomotive may be clearly heard in every part of the house, the running of two or three trains at the same time produces an effect exhilarating to the operator but less pleasing to other people, especially when they are keen on listening to the noises from some kind of polished box. Now, a railway track lies on ballast, and in providing our own track with a raised bed, we should do well to choose a material which provides quiet running. The cork, or cork-like composition, used for lining sound-proof rooms is favoured by some. Many others use felt, which may be obtained in the correct widths for single track. Roofing-felt has its friends, and there are thousands of American modellers who swear by roofing-paper, both as a general overlay and as a trackbed. Foam rubber is excellent; and baize which can be dyed will give absolutely silent running if the track is fixed a trifle loosely. Anything having the properties of a carpet is an effective sound-deadener, but before we cut up the old rug in the attic we must be sure that it will not send fluff or loose threads into the mechanism travelling over it. We also have to consider how far our old material will go, for to change the type of trackbed may bring us difficulties in track-laying besides making the layout look less attractive.

As the freshest newcomer will have realized, a sound-deadener may cover the whole surface of the baseboard, with another level for the track to rest on, or it may lie along the line of track only. A roadbed curves with the track, and so the material must be shaped accordingly. Rubber-bonded Bestikork can be curved easily to $13\frac{1}{2}$ in. radius, and felt, baize and roofing paper can be cut into curved strips. We must not forget to allow enough material for the curves; they need more than we expect, just as they need more room on the baseboard than we are apt to provide unless we plan the whole layout carefully on paper.

Our method of fastening the track depends entirely or largely upon the kind of track that we have installed. With felt, baize or any carpet-like material perfectly quiet running is best achieved by tacking down the roadbed and gluing the sleepers to it, so that the vibration of the rails is not carried straight to the baseboard underneath. But not all sleepers can conveniently be glued, and in any event the method may cause the beginner more trouble than the gain is worth.

Resorting to the standard method for our particular kind of track, we drive the spikes or screws through the roadbed into the baseboard. Our dealer, if we are in doubt, will know what fasteners we need. We do not force them through tightly. I know that we would like to make the track very rigid indeed, but this beautiful opportunity must be resisted. The track on an actual railway, though it looks immensely solid, is made to float, as the engineers say, and our model track must float also if we are to get the best results. Slightly loose pinning, in addition to reducing the noise, permits the rails to yield a little, and so promotes sweeter running of the train. It is a good idea to slip a postcard under the sleeper and then fasten the sleeper down just firmly enough for the card to be pulled out again. Points assemblies should be fixed more firmly because of the moving bar and switches, and the roadbed will have to be cut for the bar, as we see when we lay the turnout on the strip of material.

The whole layout must be linked up before we begin to design the roadbed, and must be tried out again, with the roadbed underneath, before we fix anything. In this way we detect any mistakes we have made in the paper-planning and in the cutting, together with any unevenness of the surface. As it needs only a tiny bump to derail an engine at speed, the surface on which the running rails rest must be perfectly smooth. The drawback of sectioned layouts is the joint. A latch on each side, pushed down tightly on a stud or projecting screw, will do much to close the gap if the baseboard rests solidly on the table. For the best effect, the sections are latched together and clamped to the table-top or other supporting base.

The latching device, or the hinges if a folding hinged baseboard is desired, must be fitted with great care—such care that the work is best left to a home handyman when the beginner feels that he may be unequal to it. But no one should be daunted by the task of laying a roadbed. Looking at the unrolled sheet of material, we may pick up our shears or sharp scissors with some doubt, as though we had been asked to cut out a dress. A patient, systematic approach will give us confidence. The distance between two sleepers, even on ordinary track, is not great and to draw a thin chalk line from one to another, following the run of the curve, is the worst that we have to do. The roadbed is cut a little wider than the track itself and if a solid material such as softwood is being used—for all modellers do not prefer carpeting—the sides of the bed should slope a bit to suggest the loose stuff which the platelayers, or lengthsmen, would pack in on a real line. With soft thin material the slope would not be noticeable.

One of the biggest mistakes is to stick the roadbed to the baseboard. The beginner who does this will soon regret that there was any adhesive in the house. Not only will he want to alter his layout at a later date; he will have to make various adjustments, big or small, before his present operation is finished.

Continue to experiment until you are satisfied. There is now just one more thing to be done. Send the train on its first official journey along the permanent track!

CHAPTER SEVEN

Imagination and a Map

EVERY day in summer the Elizabethan draws away from a platform at King's Cross to begin the longest regular non-stop journey on any railway in the world. Americans are astonished: England and Wales would fit into Texas five times over with enough room left for Scotland. Canadians are amazed: more than four Englands could be accommodated in Manitoba, whose vast area would easily contain Texas. Australians are unbelieving: surely one can stand at Land's End and whistle to a friend at John O' Groats?

The fact remains that the passenger who steps off the Elizabethan in Edinburgh has completed the longest unbroken railway journey on any regular service anywhere. It is just under 393 miles from the station in one capital to the station in the other. This is not the greatest distance that one can travel on a single rail trip in the tight little isle of Britain. The Caledonian, successor to the streamlined blue-and-silver Coronation Scot introduced in 1937, covers 401.4 miles (four hundred miles in four hundred minutes) on its daily runs north and south from Euston and Glasgow Central. It stops once, at the border city of Carlisle, for the Camden and Polmadie crews to be changed. The Elizabethan changes crews as it rushes along, the relief men travelling in a special compartment as far as Alne, near Leeds, and then passing through a narrow corridor in the tender (which has a small circular window) to the footplate. With a Gresley corridor tender, the Caledonian would not need to stop at Carlisle though it might still choose to do so.

These long, fast journeys are of great interest to the model railwayman. Hornby-Dublo has its own handsome Caledonian hauled by the *City of London* in British Railways maroon, the colour adopted for some of the Stanier 4-6-2

locomotives on this run. For the East Coast Route, which is famous for its expresses—above all, for the Flying Scotsman—Hornby-Dublo offers a number of suitable trains. The Talisman may be hauled by the *Golden Fleece* on two-rail track or by the record-breaking *Mallard* on the old three-rail system. Various train names and destination plates are obtainable.

To run a named train with the correct type of locomotive, also properly named, and the right destination plates on the coaches, is undoubtedly one of the thrills of railway modelling. The beginner thinks himself a lucky fellow if he has a 4-6-2 engine and can send The Caledonian through on the West Coast Route, or has a Pacific to speed The Morning Talisman north or south from King's Cross or Waverley. But the expert, much as he may delight in the appearance and performance of these trains, is compelled to object. No OO model railway, he says, can represent the run from King's Cross to Edinburgh unless the layout is a magnificent construction stretching for a little over five miles!

While this is true, I doubt if it will deter the beginner. Arguing that a model railway can never be an exact reproduction of the real thing, he can reasonably compromise with the distances, as he is forced to do with certain other aspects of the whole, and say that he is giving an impression of a famous express on its great journeys. As I pointed out before, the experts are so afraid of "playing with trains" that in condemning one absurdity they frequently suggest another. Having told us that realism is outraged when we run a four-hundred-mile express on a table-top, they proudly show us their own plans for a small-area railway: stations, locomotive sheds, automatic coalers,

complicated sidings, tunnels, cuttings, embankments, signal boxes, houses, factories, and anything else from a garage to a cathedral, all in a space which on a real railway would be a few hundred yards each way! The beginner may feel that a country is more interesting than a cricket field.

At any rate, it will be a long time before the model trains cease to pull out of London for Edinburgh or Aberdeen, Bristol or Penzance. On French layouts the Sud Express will continue to run non-stop over the 359¾ miles from Austerlitz station in Paris to St Jean in Bordeaux, and the Mistral will leave the Gare de Lyon in Paris to arrive 146 minutes later at Dijon, 195¼ miles away. Owners of American layouts, not all of them in America, will despatch the *City of Denver* on the 1,049 miles to Chicago, the Twentieth Century Limited on the 958 miles from Chicago to New York, and the Sunset Limited south-east from Los Angeles, over the border of New Mexico, across the Rio Grande, further south to San Antonio deep in the heart of Texas—and on, on to New Orleans.

The small-area plan is valuable not because it helps to solve the single problem of distance, but because it provides us with a reason for the design and working of our railway. Whatever kind of layout we have, and whatever we intend to do with it, we should work to an idea or theme. No railway exists without a reason, and our own line will be much more interesting, and much more of an intelligent unity, when we have invented a territory for it and a purpose.

Some modellers conceive of their layout as a branch line or as one of the much-loved short lines which are, alas, being closed one by one on the ground that they lose money. When the Bluebell Line in Sussex was placed on the list of victims, the daughter of a distinguished railwayman led a protest which had the support of railway lovers, model engineers and many other people. For the traveller in no need to hurry, one of the civilized pleasures of life is to ride in a train that seems to be going nowhere in particular—a tiny country train content, like the one in Aldous Huxley's *Crome Yellow*, to "creep indolently onward, goodness only knew whither, into the green heart of England".

Although these quiet, friendly little trains may seem to us as charmingly English as the maypole on the village green, other countries have them too—just as other countries (among them America) have village greens and maypoles. In Spain, Mexico and South America locomotives of incredible age wheeze from one lost village to another. The Americans have the Atchison, Topeka and Santa Fe Railway with a route length of 13,074 miles, more than half the distance round the earth at the Equator: and they also have hundreds of short lines, quite apart from the spurs which push out from the big railroads. Some of the big ones were built up from a great number of the small, as many as six hundred going to form the Pennsylvania Railroad and four hundred to create the New York Central. About twelve thousand small towns are still connected by independent short lines. Many of the towns are more like hamlets, and some are so remote that before the railway came the only way to get to any one of them was to be born there. Those large enough to be listed at all belong to the Short Line Association, which sings appealingly at meetings:

> *We're just as wide,*
> *Though not so long,*
> *And that is why,*
> *We sing this song.*

As though the official names of these concerns were not picturesque enough, they have been given nicknames more picturesque still. The Missouri and Northern Kansas is the May

Never Arrive; the Leavenworth, Kansas and Western the Leave Kansas and Walk; the Fort Smith and Western the Footsore and Weary; the Carolina and Northwestern (C and NW) the Can't and Never Will; the Newburgh, Dutchess and Connecticut the Never Did and Couldn't; the Hoosac Tunnel and Wilmington the Hoot, Toot and Whistle; and the Nevada, California and Oregon the Narrow, Crooked and Ornery; while the Maryland and Pennsylvania is of course the Ma and Pa.

The service on a backwoods short line may be irregular, and almost anything can happen. This is one of its attractions for the model railwayman. The beginner limited to a freight train may explain that the Service is "freight only"— or "mixed" when he adds a passenger coach. His tank engine does not appear out of place, and if he has an express locomotive as well he can run it occasionally on the pretext, perhaps, that it is resting from its normal duties. Waiting at a country station on the King's Cross-Cambridge line one evening, David King Martin and I had a surprise when the local train arrived. Heading it was a noble engine with a plaque on the side saying that it had travelled at 126 miles an hour. Meldreth and Melbourn, Shepreth, Foxton, Hoxton—like the humblest locomotive on a country service, *Mallard* took us from one quiet halt to the next, and at the end of the trip we spoke to the driver who cheerfully said that it was all in the day's work.

As an alternative to the short-line or branch-line plan, the beginner with an express engine can consider his layout to be a section of a main-line route on which expresses would run. But for the average beginner, with a saddle-tank or something similar, a short line offers the best opportunities. It may be a mineral railway, or a railway built to carry some other local product. This in turn may inspire the operator to fit suitable constructions—mines, quarries or factories—into the landscape. Most important of all, it provides a reason for peculiarities in the landscape and in the working of the trains. A mineral line looks perfectly natural if it runs through rough hilly country with tunnels, bridges, cuttings and a few isolated houses.

To choose an actual line as our model will take us deep into local history and give us an interest as great as the running of the model railway itself. There are variations of this idea. We may model a real line and place it in imaginary surroundings, we may build an imaginary line in real surroundings, we may have a line which is wholly imaginary, or we may blend some of these possibilities.

If we prefer a fictitious railway and a real background, we may like to copy some of the features of our own district. This is an excellent plan, but it must be carried out with skill for the results to be convincing. A better choice for the beginner is a district in another part of the country, known to him from his holidays or from reading. I particularly like the idea of a holiday railway. It deepens our interest in the district which we are visiting, encourages us to remain interested in it when we are back home, and increases our enjoyment if we return the following summer. Throughout the winter, when we give most attention to our railway, we are still re-living that wonderful week or fortnight when we felt as free as the sea-wind.

Another advantage of choosing a holiday area is that the background will probably be beautiful. Let us suppose that we are going to Cornwall. The country west of Penzance, ten miles of it, has no railway. Fortunately, it will never have one; but we can create the West Penwith Railway on our table-top, linking Mousehole and Paul and St Buryan and Sennen, and sending a line back towards St Ives through the unspoilt moorland wildness of Morvah and Zennor—not forgetting, near Land's End, the small proud town of St Just. Alternatively we

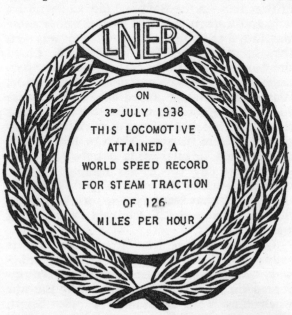

This plaque is attached to the streamlined casing of "Mallard" to commemorate its record breaking achievement.

can borrow names from other places, names such as Roseland and Rose-in-Vale, Towednack, Trink, Balnoon, Bone, Clodgy, St Winhow, Castle Bryher, Clowance, Pencairn, Amalebra, Amalveor and (if the station is long enough) Skillywadden.

There is endless inspiration for us in the Highlands or in any tract of real countryside; and not least in Wales, which is a land of little railways—though we might not think so when we come to a station with the name Llanfairpwllgwyngyllgogerychwyrndrobwllllantysiliogogogoch! But the scheme which gives us most freedom is the planning of an island railway. The island is absolutely our own. We can do just what we like there. As the towns are on or near the coast, we do not have to apologize for our continuous layout; anything else would be silly. As for our having only one engine—well, one is adequate at present. It provides a very frequent service round the islands, with inland trips on the branch line, and all the islanders are completely satisfied, which is more than many people on the mainland would say of their own local services.

We begin by drawing a map. Drawing it and pondering it will lead us further into make-believe until our island has a latitude and longitude, a history, and a name. It was in this way that the story of *Treasure Island* took shape and grew. Robert Louis Stevenson had gone to stay at Braemar—in the Balmoral district—with his wife and stepson, a boy of twelve, whose name was Lloyd Osbourne. As the weather was wet, they spent most of the time indoors. Lloyd drew and painted in the cottage, and one afternoon when he was colouring a map of a desert island his stepfather joined him, added names such as Spy-glass Hill and Skeleton Island, and then drew three red crosses to mark the hiding-place of pirate treasure. Much to Lloyd's disappointment, he afterwards took the map away—but next day Lloyd was reading the first chapter of one of the most delightful books in the world. "I have said the map was the most of the plot," wrote R.L.S. "I might almost say it was the whole."

The same may be true of our island and its railway. J. H. G. Walton and G. Y. Hemingway, two well-known railway modellers, invented the island of Cleasdale during the war when they were thousands of miles apart. Communicating by letter, they discovered all sorts of interesting things about this entirely fictitious piece of land off the Northumbrian coast. From the legends of pre-Roman Cleasdale, they carried the story on to the present. They had Latin documents and a poem *The Lament of Offa* which described a battle between the islanders and a Viking war-lord in the sixth century. The history of the Cleasdale and North Coast Railway was pieced together in detail. Secret dealings with mainland interests explained the presence of L.N.E.R. locomotives on the island, and other facts which might have seemed odd to a stranger were traced to their source in local history or geography. The council, for instance, had forbidden level crossings, thus forcing the company to dig a cutting.

To invent a place and a community is a fine exercise for the imagination and a happy training in research. Eminent people have engaged in this activity. Emily and Anne Brontë were still adding to the story of their imaginary Gondaland when Emily was twenty-seven and had written *Wuthering Heights*. A distinguished novelist of to-day has revealed how, in his youth, he played a similar game with a friend who is now a famous poet; Wingate of the Chindits, as a boy, explored the vague kingdom of Lodolf; H. G. Wells was so fond of inventing little games that he wrote two books about them; and Winston Churchill liked to fight imaginary battles with toy soldiers on the floor.

Without make-believe our lives would be cold. A model railway inspires us to engage in it with enthusiasm. We have the purpose or theme for our railway and we can develop it entertainingly until it becomes an important part of the fun. In explaining the unavoidable oddities, we are led to use our ingenuity and to weave a number of tales into one story; a narrative which, like the railway itself, has the attraction of never being complete.

We have our Gondaland. The name we give it can be anything that pleases us: Selkirk's Isle, after Alexander Selkirk who was the original of Defoe's Robinson Crusoe; Mortallone, as in Sir Arthur Quiller-Couch's *Poison Island*; or Boon Island, which provides the title of a thrilling book by Kenneth Roberts. Cocos Island would be unsuitable because of its dense tropical vegetation, but Treasure Island is not ruled out on that score—for its landscape, with the pines and oaks, seems remarkably close to Braemar. In the end, of course, we may invent a name of our own or borrow the name of our street!

CHAPTER EIGHT

The Space and the Place

WHEN is a door not a door? A young railway modeller in Hampshire has his own answer to this old and dusty riddle. "When it's a model railway!" says Brian Harvey of Basingstoke, who operates a layout in partnership with his father.

The Harvey Railway is mounted on a baseboard of plywood with a bracing underneath to prevent warping or twisting. Screws hold the track to the board, but all the taller items such as buildings and signals are removed when the railway closes for the night. Before running the trains, Brian pegs these items into small holes. The pieces using electricity have plugs attached to them so that they can be pushed into sockets linked by wires on the underside. Power from the mains is taken through a transformer and controller fixed on a small separate baseboard close to the big one, the plug at the end of a short lead fitting into a main socket in a corner outside the track.

With this system it takes only a short time to strip the layout of everything tall and to put everything back in exactly the right place when the trains are again to be run. In a few seconds the electrically-operated signals are all set to work and Pegastoke Station will light up at the touch of a switch.

As soon as the movable parts have been stowed away, the baseboard is ready to become a door. Having been made flat except for the rails and a goods platform less than an inch high, it is taken up to a bedroom. In a corner of the room stands a home-made cupboard for clothes and shoes. The cupboard has no door, but on the wall level with the open front are two sockets for hinges; and on one side of the baseboard are two hinge pins. You now know the secret. The board is lifted upright on its narrow end, the hinge pins are dropped into their sockets on the wall—and there is Brian's railway, neatly stored in a corner and at the same time serving a practical purpose as a cupboard door.

For the average house and the average small railway it would be hard to find a better arrangement. Discovering a place where we can conveniently use our layout is usually simple compared with the problem of where to put it when it is not being used. Size and shape create the first difficulty. It is not always easy to store a piece of board measuring, let us say, about six feet by four, the most popular size for the beginner. Nor, when we have found a place, is it altogether easy to take the board there and bring it back again. However small the layout, we should, for safety's sake, ask someone to help with the carrying. Even then, a base becomes awkward if its area is more than about sixteen or eighteen square feet. Sizes of four feet by four or six by three are considered the maximum for handling. This means that the workable minimum of six by four for OO gauge is rather large in one piece. If two sections are preferred, and can be fitted satisfactorily, the join should be at the longer edge.

Here is another simple procedure where we may easily go astray. The sections of an oblong baseboard should themselves be oblong. To get the measurements for each of them, halve the length of the shorter side and do nothing with the other. Supposing our baseboard to be six feet by four, half the shorter side will be two feet. The other side is not halved, and so the sections we shall order are each six feet by two.

Instead of having a portable baseboard, the owner of a table-sized railway sometimes uses the bare table-top and adds a hinged board to form a drop-leaf. The hinged side should again be the longer one. It is not essential for the flap to run the whole length of the table. A square not in itself big will extend the running area surprisingly and provide room for a curve that would be too large for the ordinary table-top. So useful is the L-shaped base that Trix manufacture two table-top units which will fit together in this form, the main unit measuring five feet by three-and-a-half and the extension unit five feet by two.

Hinging a fixed baseboard increases the running area; hinging a portable one reduces the space needed for storage and makes the layout easier to move—easier, that is to say, when the taller pieces on the board are not in danger of being crushed. This problem may be solved in the actual carrying by fixing little bars at the ends so that they connect the two sections at the corners and, like the supports for the lid of a gramophone (using a pair from an old gramophone might be considered) prevent one part from falling on the other. But this does not remove the difficulty of storing the layout in limited space. On the contrary, it creates the further difficulty that any construction on the upright part is left clinging, as it were, to the side of a cliff. The only solution is to remove all the items except the track; and the best way of doing it is by the pegging system, as on the Harvey Railway.

The join remains a drawback. While many model railwaymen have overcome this snag without tears, the beginner who is more or less compelled to use sections will prefer those which fit edge to edge, through the use of latches or, what is better, two rows of pegs and sockets. For the track to be laid permanently on both sections, the join must be so snug that it is almost invisible. The desirability of avoiding the occurrence of more than one join at the same place is not to be regarded as a rule—who cares, so long as the running is satisfactory?—but it is generally important to have the points at least a few inches (three may be enough) from the dividing-line between sections.

Layouts are stored in every imaginable place and in places most of us would not think of at all. Some boys and men sleep with their railways; the layout reposes close to them: under the bed, between the head of the bed and the wall, or in the nearest corner. A fence or wall around the baseboard will protect it from damage but not from dust. It also looks slightly out of place when the railway is assembled, unless the supports are pegged into holes and can be removed before the running begins. The best protection, the only complete one, is a box. It can be very shallow indeed or it can be deep enough to hold the layout in running order. Nothing is better than a box stored flat with all the items fixed for the next tour of duty. Resting on battens, or on two side strips, the baseboard will itself form the bottom, while a second section may, if desired, drop into place as the lid. Tapes attached to the underside of the board are useful for lifting it out of the box.

Applied differently, the same idea gives us a cabinet. This method of storage has two advantages. The entire equipment, including the trains, can be packed together, with room for other accessories as they are added. More important, a well-made cabinet can stand in any room of the house, thus enabling us to keep the railway in the sitting room or dining room close to where we operate. In some houses the model railwayman can pack and unpack without crossing the room: he takes his railway out of the cabinet and runs it on the top.

Lucky are those for whom space is not a problem: the people with spare rooms, big dry lofts, disused barns, and garages where a bubble-car sits proudly in an area ample for a Rolls-Royce. For the beginner who has a room to himself the commoner difficulties do not arise. His problem is how to make the best use of great opportunities!

In a spare room the layout may rest on any support that is reasonably sturdy and of a suitable height—normally about three feet or three and a half. An old kitchen table is ideal for a small railway which is keeping to its present bounds. But few houses to-day have any spare furniture, and the beginner in need of an old table must usually buy one. Before he takes this course he should consider getting a cheap, simple new table instead. I advise him to call at the local Do-It-Yourself shop. He may come back with a table under his arm! Two long and two short pieces of wood fit into slots at the top of each leg to form a rigid whole. To complete an ordinary table one lays a sheet of hardboard on the framework, but when the table is for a model railway the baseboard may itself be the top. The beginner therefore buys just what he needs: a rigid frame at table-height to support his layout. As soon as the railway expands, another table may be placed close against the first. Before this is done the position of the legs should be noted. If they slope—and usually it is

Above : George Heiron's painting of the Merchant Navy Class "Holland-America Line" leaving Salisbury.

Below : Viaduct built by Guy Williams, a Bristol teacher, for the Pendon EM Railway.

the sharp angle of the legs which hold the parts so firmly—the second top or baseboard must be long enough to cover the space between the V created when the tables are placed together with legs touching at the bottom. Here, too, it is worth while to experiment with an L.

The use of fix-it-yourself tables is similar to the old and popular arrangement of a railway supported by trestles. With either method the trackage may be extended indefinitely and the base may be of any straight-sided shape: a long rectangle like one of the tables at a Sunday School treat, an L, a double-L, an E (the double-L with another piece in the middle) or a complete square: not to mention variations on these designs, such as a T, a double-T, or even, where there is room, a Z with an upright backbone. A design may be entirely changed without much trouble and without altering the long straight lengths of main-line track. Moving the position of a trestle table provides us, in effect, with a new layout once the alterations have been made in the areas where the tables join. At the gap between tables, or between any two sections of layout, we may use a short length of track which can be lifted and laid down again with less bother than a unit of the full length.

Most clubs, and many private operators of the more advanced railway, build their own structures. The commonest kind is a bench of the desired height and width. When it occupies the main area of a room, the shape preferred is a square or oblong, rather like four tables placed at right angles to make a stall at a garden fête, with the stallholders on the inside. This is the easiest arrangement for controlling the railway.

A popular alternative, adopted by clubs and by private owners, is the bench-along-the-wall layout. Keeping the track to the sides of a room leaves all the rest of the area free. Some boys run a wall railway in the bedroom and are still able to go to bed and get up, like other people. For those fortunate enough to have a spare room the arrangement is excellent as it leaves plenty of space for other agreeable activities, including the construction of railway buildings and scenery.

The structure will be narrow, except in a loft whose sloping roof forces us to stand farther back from the walls. Once the bench is built, we want to use the entire length of it for running. Our ambition is to send a train right around the room—even across the doorway, where we

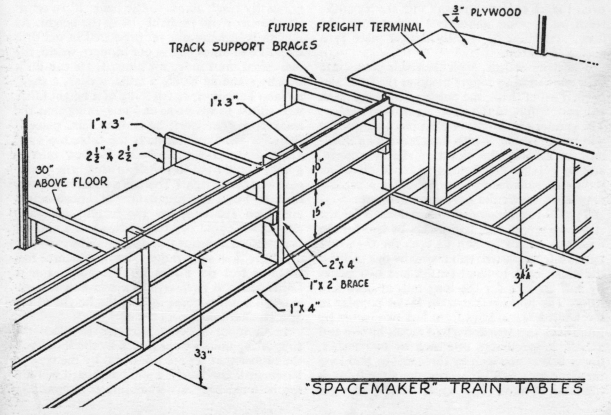

"SPACEMAKER" TRAIN TABLES

shall have a section that lifts like a drawbridge. What a thrill that is, to watch a train travelling all the way along the walls! I doubt if we shall lay double track until we have the longest running-table we can construct, and the longest permanent way. All our track for a good while to come will be devoted to this long, exciting single-line.

We can think of the supporting framework as a series of connected tables. The material may be of deal or of any wood suitable for a construction which is not intended to be a masterpiece of beauty. Old wood will suffice, but when there is none of it to hand the far more sensible choice is new wood from the shop, already cut to the right sizes.

While the structure should be firm, it need not be so strong as the old-fashioned experts tell us. Each table or section has the usual four legs, and so long as they serve their usual purpose we shall not bother about their exact size. Advanced modellers like them to be two inches by two, as on a kitchen table, but it may not be necessary to have them quite so thick. They are kept upright by side-pieces which also may not need to be so big as the recommended size, two inches wide and an inch thick. One piece connects the leg close to the wall with the leg at the front, at a point about two inches from the floor. A similar or slightly thicker piece runs across at the top.

The pairs of legs, with their side-pieces, are then connected by longer pieces at the front and back. Two of them, the pair on which the track will rest, will hold the structure firmly together. The greater the length of each piece the solider will be the whole. Width does more than thickness in keeping the structure rigidly upright, and to get the full benefit of it we place the screws or nails (screws are better) in a vertical row when we fix the horizontal supports.

Typical recommended measurements for the structure are, in full, two inches by two for the legs, two inches by half an inch for the lower back-to-front batten, two inches by one inch for the upper back-to-front batten, and two inches by half an inch for the long rails at back and front. The Spacemaker train tables popular in the United States have front legs two inches by four, back legs two and a half inches by two and a half, lower braces one inch by two inches, upper braces one inch by three inches, and long rails one inch by four inches along the front at top and bottom. The upper braces, at right

angles to the wall, support the track. Below them, on the smaller braces, rests a platform or shelf, its underside fifteen inches above the upper edge of the floor rail.

In normal conditions a framework built to either of these sets of measurements will stand rigidly without further bracing. As I have suggested, the beginner may be able to vary them in the interests of economy. Once again, a good deal depends on the circumstances. A bench extending from corner to corner of a room, and fitting tightly into the space, will be kept from swaying by the wall at either end.

Corrections will have to be made when the floor is uneven. These are necessary, not only because we want the baseboard to be level for the track, but also because a stiff level baseboard will not fit properly if the supports are at various levels. A little cardboard neatly inserted here and there may provide the adjustment. Laid under the baseboard, corrugated cardboard has the virtue of reducing noise.

The width of the framework is decided by our general plans for the railway balanced against what we are actually able to do. Unless we have plenty of space and plenty of wood we are not likely to build it too wide—so wide that we cannot easily reach across to the back. If we err at all, the error will probably be in the height. As human beings are not yet produced in uniform sizes like so much else in our modern world, the individual must judge for himself. He can do it best by standing beside a table, a desk, a shelf, a piano keyboard, or anything of a height fairly well suited to his own, and imagining that the track is at that level; he can, in fact, place it there for the experiment. Is the table too low? Does the sink-board in the kitchen offer a guide? Would the top shelf of this little bookcase be exactly right? There is a tendency nowadays to build the foundation at breast-height and even eye-level, but the heights generally chosen are about two feet or two and a half for the junior enthusiast (though many boys to-day are taller than their fathers) and from three feet to three feet six inches for the adult. For a father-and-son partnership, a convenient aver-average is thirty-three inches, the height of the Spacemaker tables.

In deciding at what intervals to place the supporting units we are guided by the solidity of the timber that we are using and by the type of baseboard. Obviously, a stiff baseboard will not sag between supports which are comparatively far apart—five feet or more. With another type, not so stiff, the distance may be two feet or three. A simple test gives us the answer.

We must make the most of the long pieces as the overall supports which keep the legs upright and brace the entire framework. The fixing at each leg, as I have indicated, should be firm. It is best for the end of each piece to lie flat across the whole width of the leg. The next length to be fitted is then placed just above it and taken straight along to another leg where the third long piece will be fixed just *below* it at the same level as the first. This staggered arrangement looks attractive as well as improving the structure.

Whether screws or nails are used, I strongly recommend the addition of glue. A silly and misleading prejudice against modern adhesives exists among older men who are themselves skilled carpenters. It explains the heaviness of their constructions and their difficult designs, with carpenters' joints and unnecessary bracing. We are not building a platform for a troupe of Cossack dancers, and with the help of glue we can make a running-table which is simple, light and adequately strong. This applies to all our constructions and is worth bearing in mind when we work to the published designs of some of the older experts.

All wood should be seasoned and dry and is the better for a coat of paint or stain, though we shall be reluctant to spend time on this work when we are eager for the first train to pull out. Painting is particularly advisable in any room with a tendency to dampness. A moist atmosphere also affects the buildings and other structures on a model railway, besides doing no good to the track. For this reason the gear should not be stored in a loft or cellar unless the place is known to be dry.

The more carefully our running-table is built the better it will stand and the better it will look. I have seen admirable layouts on foundations so crude and messy that half the charm was lost. The under-part provides a useful place for storage, especially if shelves are fitted. Shelves help to strengthen the framework, but they do nothing to improve its appearance when they are littered with odds-and-ends. The effect of a well-built foundation may be ruined by visible untidiness, and the pleasure which a spectator receives from the orderliness of the tracks and the realism of the scenery is greatly weakened by the contrast.

I have likened a model railway to a modern painting but it resembles even more a theatrical performance. We have had in this century many strange plays: a play in which the characters speak their secret thoughts; a play in which the audience is asked to throw its chairs on to the stage to keep a fire burning; a play with two characters who live in dustbins; and almost everything else imaginable except a play (surely we can expect it soon?) whose characters throw bags of soot at the audience. In one or two of these works the back-stage arrangements are brought to the front: carpenters come on to change the scenery while the players are talking. Such originality does not deserve to be imitated. If our layout is a stage, we shall be old-fashioned and hide what normally belongs behind the scenes.

Boarding or curtains at the front (the boarding, of course, brings us back to the idea of a cabinet) will let the railway speak for itself without rude shouts from below. But this belongs to the future. Indeed, our whole plan for a spare-room type of railway belongs there, except for those of us who have the opportunity to install a bigger layout now. In trying to help these lucky ones, the fortunate few in each district who number a great many across the world, I have deliberately jumped ahead, for nothing encourages the beginner more than a forward look and the knowledge of what he may achieve in time.

CHAPTER NINE

Patterns to Follow

THOUGH few of us have ever been inside a railway signal box we all know what we should see there. That long soldierly row of levers is familiar to us from early childhood: even girls are able to recognize it. But the time is coming when this picture will be a peep into the past. Here and there on a quiet branch line, if there are any quiet branch lines left, we shall discover the shirt-sleeved operator standing in front of his signal frame while a surviving steam engine chuffs contentedly by; but everywhere else the signalman, like the driver of a diesel-electric locomotive, will be seated at a desk.

Electricity has long been used in railway signalling. Until recent years the instructions sent by this means were for the signalmen themselves: messages by telegraph and, much more frequently, the messages which come through as strokes on a bell—such as four beats for "Is the line clear?" The next development was bound to be the all-electric signal-box. We have it now, rather belatedly, as part of the modernization of British Railways.

The levers in an all-electric box are tiny enough to be worked by finger and thumb. Above the control-desk small lamps on a diagram light up to show the position of every vehicle in the area. At York, in a box which cost half a million pounds, one frame takes the place of 867 mechanical levers and sets a road, as the signalmen say, for 827 different routes. In the box at Chaloner's Whin Junction, where the Leeds and London lines meet, the work is done by only twelve route-switches on the signalling panel—but the relay room contains four hundred miles of wire.

Flicks of the thumb control both signals and points. At last, then, the real railways are beginning to catch up with the miniature ones,

for the ease of working enjoyed by the modern signalman in a few expensive boxes has been common to the simplest model layouts for many years past. The manual control of points and signals is favoured on the whole not by the beginner, as a stranger to the hobby might expect, but by the more experienced modeller. It is he, with his greater desire for realism, who insists on mechanical operation, happily accepting all the complications of manual levers and lineside pull-wires. The beginner, backing away from the probability of a wild and unworkable tangle, prefers the simplicity of a hand-lever right at the spot, and is delighted with the still greater simplicity of electrical remote-control. As modernization expands, the railway modeller eager to keep abreast of full-scale practice will therefore have to simplify and catch up with the amateur!

Installing manual control of signals and turnouts at a distance is the most difficult project in railway modelling. The brass rodding, nickel-silver wire, piano wire, waxed thread, or whatever is used to connect the levers in the signal-box with the final levers, must be run beside the track in such a way that it will move; it must be taken around corners if the material is flexible; and it must be of exactly the right length. After everything has been fixed, further difficulties may be expected. Sooner or later the thread (No. 24 black is the favourite) will either break or stretch, while the rodding or wire may be sometimes too long and sometimes too short, according to the changes in temperature which cause metal to expand and contract. The gradual stretching of the thread, or a variation in temperature, often has a lesser effect, especially on a small layout, than the constant shifting which occurs on every baseboard. By this I mean, not the alterations carried out by the

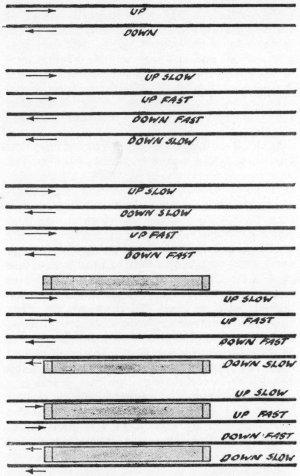

becomes a pull at the other end. But the other rod is also pushing, its expansion being in the opposite direction. The two movements are equal, and so the expansion makes no difference.

Charming though this device is, we shall be content with the simpler methods of operation. Once we have a couple of turnouts laid down, we realize that the manual operation of points is going to keep us busy. It is well that we learn this early. The worst and commonest error in railway modelling is the tendency to overcrowd. It springs from the belief that the more one packs on to the baseboard the more "complete" will be the railway. What would we think of an artist who worked on such a principle?

The modeller who wants an attractive, realistic and fully workable railway must learn the art of leaving out. Adding bits for the sake of adding them will make his layout less of a railway than it was when all the parts would go into a cereal box. Not a few model railways are spoilt by sheer enthusiasm, by such an urge to build and improve that the limit of actual need is reached, passed, and left far behind. "Is your journey really necessary?" was a question asked on thousands of posters in Britain during the war. "Is this addition really necessary?" should be asked and answered by the model railwayman before he buys or makes any new item.

The time soon arrives when our layout, which once looked woefully bare, faces the danger of containing too much. At a stage where there is still plenty of room for buildings and other structures, the track tends to be congested and complicated. Despite our keenness for points, we hesitate after the third or fourth pair. We now understand, as we may not have understood earlier, that very few points can or should be placed on the main lines. Our attention therefore turns, naturally and properly, to the sidelines. It is at the sidings, as we discover, that points can be used to the greatest benefit of the railway and with the greatest pleasure to ourselves.

With two, three or four pairs of points the temptation may be strong to complicate the working unnecessarily. All sorts of tricks can be worked with points. But there are no tricks on a real railway. The full-scale systems were not designed to amuse the engineers, bewilder the signalmen, and impress the public. If the complications of track at a big station or junction look like a puzzle, this is because the operations there are complicated for sound and clear

operator—though these, too, are important—but the more or less invisible bending and creeping that takes place. Ghostly as it may seem, the wood of the base moves a tiny bit; while the metal on the layout, besides changing a little in length, yields a fraction with use. The total result after a while is a shift not big enough to be obvious, but big enough to affect an adjustment which has to be precise.

To compensate for variations in the length of control-line, expert modellers adopt a bright idea which is, like nearly everything ingenious, really simple. The rodding is broken at the halfway point, and the two ends thus formed are attached to opposite ends of a bar which turns on a pivot in the middle. When the rods expand, their ends push forward—like the ends of a running-rail, where the platelayers on an actual railway leave a gap. As the bar is at the halfway point, the expansion of the two lengths is the same. Now, a push at one end of the bar reasons. What the railways want, and what they are planning to achieve with the new methods and conditions, is greater simplicity wherever this improvement is possible. There used to be forty-four levers in the signal-box at Chaloner's Whin Junction. The twelve thumb-switches replace them, and the total number of signals is a mere five.

With or without modernization, the underlying pattern of a railway is always simple in the sense that every aspect of the working, taken separately, has a definite purpose and is reasonably straightforward. Allowing as usual for the exceptions, nothing is complicated needlessly.

First we have the main lines. They connect the principal stations and carry through-trains. The track may be single, double, or whatever the traffic demands. In Britain it is usual to have an Up line and a Down, and the left-hand road as the driver sees it is the proper running road. American trains, like American cars, keep to the right, but on great lengths of main-line two trains cannot pass as the track is single. On a country branch-line in Britain—a typical single-track—the signals may be at junctions only. Other one-track routes are signalled both ways, the traffic being normally Up and Down.

Branch lines are of course the off-shoots leading to smaller places in the area. Occasionally a fair-sized or important town may be served— as, for example, Lincoln, which objected to the railway and has been on a branch line ever since. Such lines are sometimes single-track. In general their equipment is comparatively simple.

Duplicate, slow or relief lines are known to all of us, by sight if not by name. They are the extra lines placed beside the main Up and Down for use when traffic is heavy. Some are reserved as far as possible for local passenger and goods trains—which is why we commonly speak of them as the Slow Lines. They may run together at the side of the main road, so that they suggest a small separate railway (the original line) or they may be separated, with the fast lines between—a plan worth considering for a model railway, as two platforms will serve all four roads. At stations the slow and fast lines are connected.

Loop, avoiding, or independent lines are best described by the first of these three names. The loop line at a station, or between stations, provides a bay where a slow train such as the average freight may wait for a fast train to pass, and then go forward again to rejoin its original track. Each end is therefore connected with the main track by a turnout. A train runs through more easily when the two turnout curves are parallel (so that the loop has a lopsided look in a diagram) but the curves on a passing loop between stations may be arranged the other way (the outline resembling a shallow pan) as the train, being free of station urgencies, is able to enter the loop more slowly. It is easy to find the exact opposite of this, as of almost anything else which is common in full-scale practice.

Reception lines and refuge sidings are similar to ordinary loops, but in different ways. The reception line accommodates the goods train before and after the trucks have been sorted out, or marshalled. It generally looks like an ordinary loop, whereas the refuge siding is a spur which has exactly the same purpose as a loop in that it allows a train to turn off and wait while another train passes. The difference lies in the dead-end of the siding. Connection with the main track being at one point only, the train

Contemporary-styled signal box at Balham, London.

using a refuge sidings has to back, an awkward and dangerous practice which is not much liked. The modeller who converts his refuge sidings into a loop is following full-scale example.

Safety-points, catch-points or derailing switches—we remember Dyke in our first chapter—are placed at loops, sidings and other points where collisions are most likely to occur. To throw a runaway vehicle off the track, and away from the main running line, the railways install a turnout with a single tongue or with a single tongue and a deflecting rail. This device will derail a runaway moving toward the traffic line at a slow or moderate speed, according to the slope. For higher speeds, as when part of a goods train breaks away and tears down a hill, the points are of the ordinary kind except that the inside rail ends in a wood block. The sounds which a signalman least likes to hear is the five-pause-five bell telling him that a train has run away. This happens from time to time with freights, and will continue to happen until all freight rolling stock is fitted with continuous brakes as passenger vehicles have been, by law, for the past seventy years. On one occasion, when a visiting inspector was spending the night at the home of a country stationmaster, the wagons of a passing freight became detached, ran down a hill and up the other side, and then swung down-and-up, down-and-up, in a kind of pendulum movement, the buffers crashing together at intervals. "I had no idea," said the inspector when he came down to breakfast in the morning, "that you had so much traffic on this line"!

Sand-drags are rails placed beside the ordinary running line in a steel or wooden trough filled with sand or gravel so that the wheels of the runaway churn in the loose material until the increasing friction brings them to a standstill. To provide for possible break-aways in the Vale of Neath, where a gradient extends for a mile and five yards, the railway introduced a sand drag a thousand feet long and tested it with a coal train weighing over a thousand tons. At thirty-three miles an hour the train was stopped in thirty-two seconds; and afterwards two engines were needed to haul it out again. This admirable device was invented by an Austrian engineer, Kopcke of Dresden, and was first used in England by the London and North Western Railway in the tunnel between Edge Hill and Waterloo Dock, Liverpool.

As safety switches are required on real rail-

Typical English signal box built about 30 years ago.

ways under Government regulations, the advanced modeller will install them—but only for the sake of appearance. The beginner will not bother with them at all. Staging a collision, or a derailment to prevent a collision, is one of the many temptations that the amateur has to avoid, for the mechanism of the most robust model vehicle is none the better for violent treatment on or off the line.

Double junctions, flying junctions and burrowing junctions are other features of the railway that belong in the main to the more highly developed layout. The double junction is a possible exception. It occurs when a double-line branches off, and it may therefore be incorporated by the beginner who decides to have double-track. The flying junction carries the diverging tracks over the main line on bridges, thus avoiding what is known in America as a grade crossing, and the burrowing junction has the diverging tracks at an ordinary level and the main-line lower, with the use of cuttings and a tunnel. These arrangements, which can provide spectacular effects, are commonest at points where electric trains must keep to their own lines without crossing other lines on the level. They are extremely expensive to build—in money for the railways and in space for the modeller.

All the other features fit naturally and easily into our plans.

CHAPTER TEN

Track Problems are Fun

AS most model railways—let us be honest about it—provide a continuous run, and as the run is as long as the size of the base permits, expansion is usually towards the wide open spaces of the interior. There may be opportunities at the corners, and on both sides of the main track when a different design of layout is chosen, but on most table-top railways the branch lines and sidings run inward with the main lines forming a border.

To the size and shape of this area our plans must be adapted. We want to use it in such a way that we shall enjoy a variety of operations without doing anything that would be seriously out-of-place, or completely crazy, on a full-sized railway. It is one of our ambitions to use as many interesting devices as we can get: points, diamond crossovers, turntables and the like. We may not be able to fit all of these into a sensible pattern, for each of them, as I remarked earlier, takes up a fair amount of room. It is just as well, perhaps, that we cannot afford everything in the manufacturers' catalogues. As it is, our natural wish to add all that we can must yield to these two limiting factors, lack of space and the demands of realism. It is difficult not to harp on realism because the degree of our respect for it is the distance between a toy and a model. Summing it all up in a few words, I would say: use all the facilities you can, but do not use any one of them purely for its own sake. Let us now consider the purpose and use of these devices.

First we have our turnouts. With more pairs of points we are able to send the train off in a clockwise direction and bring it back anti-clockwise on the same continuous line without putting the engine into reverse, lifting it from the track, or employing a turntable. A plain oval will send the train eastward along one

straight side and westward along the other, but this is not the complete reverse that we are seeking.

If we run a train on to a branch-line or spur, the only extension possible with a single turnout, we can return it to the main line operation-

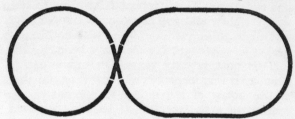

SIMPLE USE OF DIAMOND CROSSING

OVAL AND HALF OVAL; TWO TURNOUTS

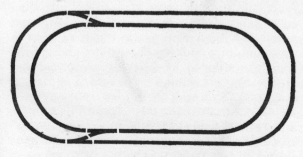

TWO OVALS WITH TWO CROSSOVERS

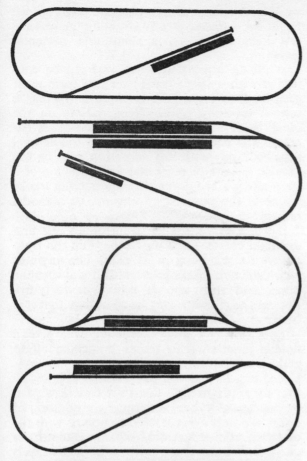

eliminate the cross-connection of track. Branching off at a left-hand turnout, the train completes a loop-circuit and re-enters the main-line through the second left-hand turnout with the engine pointing the opposite way. Two right-hand turnouts produce a similar effect. But this bulbous-shaped loop is too large and awkward for most beginners: it forms in effect a second layout.

In addition, a straight run through an ordinary reversing-loop is not possible unless the direction of the train agrees with the points. If a train travelling clockwise through a pair of facing points turns anti-clockwise on the loop, it obviously cannot turn off at the points again except by backing. Consequently only one change of direction can be made on a non-stop run.

A different effect is achieved by sending the train through an end-loop. The engine may go right or left round the loop, according to the route set by the points, but its direction at the exit from the loop, where it rejoins the straight track, will always be the same. Place a loop at either end of a straight run. A westbound train reaches the points at the entrance to the western loop. Whether it goes right ahead or is switched by the points, it still follows the curve back to the straight. It becomes an eastbound train. Then, on running through the loop at the other end, it begins a second trip westward. The movements repeat themselves, with the difference that the swing on the two loops may sometimes be one way and sometimes the other, as we decide. These changes are interesting for a time, but eventually the repetitions bore us and we either discard the end-loops or use them as the basis of a design which gives more variety. As a basic pattern the end-loop is of great value.

The simplest design for a single oval is one which incorporates a spur and allows the engine to enter the circuit on either a right curve or a left as the operator decides. This may be done most neatly by using a Y turnout. Hornby had a Y turnout before the war and it was much appreciated by modellers in Britain and America as an excellent device for reversing locomotives (by joining the branching lengths) without a turntable and in a small area. "Why no wye?" is a question sadly asked by many until they find what they want in the catalogues of the non-proprietary tracks.

We can provide the equivalent of a Y by using ordinary turnouts, but this arrangement is

ally only by reversing it. On backing out from the branch, the engine will still face in the direction that it would have taken had it not turned off. Even when we have our second turnout, the problem of escaping from this limitation is still without a satisfactory solution. A loop with a different kind of turnout at each end leaves us as we were, for the train must either run forward through the loop and continue on the main-line as before, or it must back into the loop, an operation which again makes no difference to its original direction when it resumes its journey, whether from the entrance to the loop or from the exit at the other end.

A solution is found in the installation of two turnouts of the same kind. A loop snaking across the inside of an oval from one left-hand or right-hand turnout to another will change a clockwise run to anti-clockwise, or the other way about, but this kind of connection is sometimes undesirable on an electric track as it may cause permanent short-circuiting. The alternative of a reversing loop outside the oval will more cumbersome than may at first be realized. Possibly we shall return to the idea of an outside loop if we can afford the space. A reversing loop at least gives us the pleasure of an extra running area. It is in fact extremely popular on advanced layouts, especially with the point-to-point enthusiast who insists on the best of both worlds: a straight, realistic run with the advantage of a return journey as on a continuous track. Sometimes the loop is hidden in a corner, behind scenery, or right at the rear, behind a painted backcloth. This bit of deception is forgivably part of a model railwayman's stagecraft!

All these problems, which are part of the fun, solve themselves as we progress and can see for ourselves, with the equipment before us, what we are able or unable to do within the limits of our working area—and our pocket. We must continue to plan, and the planning, for safety's sake, should be on paper; or on cardboard, the actual shapes then being fitted into the layout as a test. The planning is itself an entertainment, not unlike that which we get from mathematical puzzles (out of school); it also increases the pleasure of anticipation when we are about to add the new piece of track.

With two turnouts we can have a half-oval outside our original one, so that there are three straight tracks parallel, two of them well apart. The addition of uncoupling rails makes this layout immensely more interesting than a plain oval, but a still better design is obtained by using the two turnouts for spurs leading to terminal stations or to one terminal station and a siding. It is worth while to allow enough space for a spur and a terminal station at diagonally opposite corners of the baseboard—north-east —let us say, and south-west. As an alternative, both stations are placed at the same end, east or west, an arrangement which looks slightly less natural but makes for ease of control. In the interests of realism the ends of the line should not be close together, and for the sake of smooth running a straight run should separate the turnouts, wherever convenient, so that the train has a chance to recover from one pair of points, as it were, before it meets the next pair. When the end-stations are relatively close, it can be assumed that there is at least one through-station on the circuit to give the train a reason for its roundabout journey. This is still more important with a single terminal station. The train must be bound for a distant station, unless

we intend to run scenic pleasure tours as we might do, without greatly straining the observer's imagination, on a small and romantic island.

While an outer and inner oval can be connected with a single cross-over, the train must then back to regain the outer line, whereas a second crossover (with facing points on the inner oval) will make the exit as easy as the entry. The beginner considering a double-oval may be happy with this limitation until he has another couple of turnouts; for the swing of a train along a crossover between parallel tracks is one of the prettiest movements on a model railway.

It will also delight us to introduce our first diamond crossing and watch the train run right across a track lying in its path. The angle at which the two tracks intersect is not always the same, and with one of ninety or forty-five degrees the crossing may be so bumpy that it is better avoided.

Two turnouts and a crossing will give a double junction (two tracks branching off to make a total of four), and two double junctions placed end to end will provide a double crossover for transferring a fast train to a slow road or vice versa. At some crossings the addition of a slip, a points arrangement combined with the diamond, allows the train to change course from one interesecting route to the other. The slip is inside or outside the diamond according to the angle. But the beginner is not much concerned with this device, or with the use of movable frogs for the greater safety of fast trains; both facilities belong to the highly developed railway with scale track.

A circle and oval may be connected by a diamond crossing, but the figure of eight so formed soon loses its interest unless turnouts and side-lines are introduced to break the monotony of a circuit which is all too simple. In Tri-ang this design requires twenty standard radius curves, four half-curves, two straights and, of course, the diamond. One power clip is sufficient.

Fitted together, two crossovers and a diamond produce a scissors crossover. One pair of turnouts is right-hand and the other left hand, with the diamond at the meeting place of the two curves. A train travelling in either direction, east or west, can cross to the parallel track.

When the advanced modeller needs to construct a complete crossover in a short length, as at a terminal station, he employs a points assembly whose two roads curve out from each other. These parallel points, as they are called were once found in Hornby but have now vanished. They can be made from flexible track or by manipulating ordinary track if one is able to fit a short or cut reverse-curve on to the curved part of a turnout and another cut curve on to the straight part.

With scale flexible track we can make the devices, including the Y, not obtainable in the proprietary systems such as Hornby-Dublo, Tri-ang and Trix. We can also achieve better effects in general—curves of larger radius and turnouts where the swing is less abrupt. Best of all is the improvement in appearance.

The track is cut to length with a Junior hacksaw, a jeweller's saw, or a Trix X-acto saw, and is curved to the required radius by gentle bending after the web under the rails themselves has been cut at intervals. Spikes hold it to the baseboard. One length is fixed to the next by fish-plates, rail joiners or soldering, as explained in the leaflets supplied. When a length is bent into a curve, the inner rail sticks out at the end and the protruding piece has to be chopped off.

Wiring for any kind of two-rail track is simple. We need not be amateur electricians to understand that a gap at any point in the track will isolate electrically all the track beyond it. This cutting-off is put to a positive use in the operation of two trains on the same layout and in the automatic stopping of a train at a turn-out where the switches are against it. In short, the track is sectioned. When, for instance, a half-oval is joined to an oval by a turnout at either end, a train may be isolated in the loop while another operates normally in the main oval.

On being fed to the track at the facing or blade end of the points, the current flows only in the direction to which the points are set, and so the route is fixed electrically by the current as well as mechanically by the actual movement of the points. A train not intended to pass through will be completely unable to go any further and will thus be saved from derailment.

Sectioning is always a help, for anyone may easily forget a switch or remember it a little too late. The single operator of more than one train finds it a great convenience in handling the traffic. He can hold one train while he is sending another through or is making it up in the siding.

Hornby-Dublo has an isolating rail which is particularly useful in sidings work. By means of it the operator may construct a buffer-stop section, adding an uncoupling rail to detach the engine, which is then drawn forward into the isolated section and switched out. An un-coupling rail frequently plays a part in the isolating strategy for any part of the track. The exact placing of the rail is discovered by experiment.

Sectioning is also achieved by inserting insulating tabs—pieces of thin card are sufficient—between gaps in the current-bearing rails. When power is supplied to a continuous layout at the facing end of points it will feed back round the circuit to the trailing end, thus undoing the good work, unless a tab is provided to break the flow.

Because of the gaps, a fairly simple layout may require two power clips. These needs are determined by the extent to which we are in effect combining two or more separate layouts. Our half-oval loop, and our circle and oval with a diamond connecting them, will each operate with one power clip, but when we place one oval inside another and join the two by crossovers we need a couple of power clips, as the degree

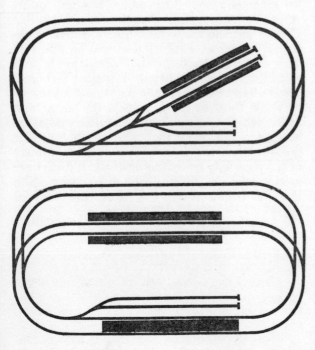

of virtual separation with four turnouts involved is obviously greater.

The function of loops and turnouts may be performed, at the correct places, by a turntable. Can we resist one? We need no excuse for getting it. A device which swings a railway engine in its own length is as useful as it is attractive: useful for reversing an engine or for switching it to another track. The first of these purposes appeals to the beginner who wants a simple way of sending his train back in the opposite direction. To turn the engine through a half circle is fun. But the rest of the train remains as it was, and so the engine has to push chimney-first. This is not a highly desirable operation when it has to be carried out with every other train. Odder still is the problem created at the other end when the train, having arrived with the engine last, must depart on its next journey with the engine pulling in reverse. In the end, we have achieved a roundabout method of reversing with emphasis on the roundabout!

Installed on the plainest type of layout, a turntable will produce a remarkably eccentric railway. Its correct and only convenient place is off the main-line, in the engine yard. It should be regarded purely as a device for turning a single vehicle and not as a movable section of the running-line. The train-reversing operation is seldom easy if the detached engine is to rejoin the waiting carriages or wagons in the ordinary chimney-first pulling position.

We must therefore beware of getting a turntable before we are ready for it. Placed in the station area, with a set of short tracks leading back to a real or imaginary engine shed, it will act as the equivalent of several turnouts. An engine which enters the shed in reverse is ready to go out again chimney-first to the main-line.

The turntables on an actual railway operate in a cavity. It may be a pit deep enough for the girders to be below ground level, or a shallow pit in which the girders are above the surface; and it may be open or closed. The bridge usually turns on a pivot at the centre, and has small wheels running on a rail at the circumference and on inner circles as well if further support is needed—as it is when the engine is a modern giant. Some American locomotives are so long that they cannot be accommodated even on a turntable a hundred feet in diameter. Wherever possible a system of points is used instead.

In real practice as in modelling, the method of turning varies. The motive power may be supplied by the driver and firemen, both pushing. We are told that in this way a hundred-ton locomotive can be turned with ease; but the ease is more apparent to the observer than to the men who are doing the work. A better method uses a wheel which is turned by hand at the side, but even this is primitive compared with the system at the bigger stations where all the effort is left to a motor driven either by electricity or by air. The air comes from the engine itself, the vacuum-brake pipe having a hose taken to it from a tall standpipe on the control platform.

In earlier days, the turntable occupied the centre of an engine shed which was curved. In time the railways came to favour a rectangular shed so that the engines might have a straight run through from a yard at the front to another at the rear. But the buildings were still known as round-houses. The name has an oddly romantic ring "Los Angeles called to San Diego and Barstow that the Southern California engineers might know and be ready in their lonely round-houses." Perhaps in our minds some hint is stirred of ancient forts and castles. However that may be, it must please us to know that the newest sheds are being built in the old shape, as a curved building takes up less space at a depot than a strictly oblong one holding the same number of engines. Whatever of the past may be lost to us as the railways are modernized, we have at least the compensation that the round-houses are to be really curved again.

CHAPTER ELEVEN

Change Here for Greyfriars

SHOULD the railways be abolished? Crazy though this question sounds to us, there are numbers of reasonably sane people who would answer it with a loud and confident 'Yes'. Their argument is that the railway has outlived its time. In the nineteenth century, as an improvement on horse-transport, it had a great part to play; in an age of aircraft and fast cars it is hopelessly out-of-date. The diesel-electric locomotive belongs in a museum with the steam engine, for the whole conception of the iron road is itself antique. Instead of spending huge sums on trying to modernize what can never be modern, let us use these millions to convert the permanent way into long straight motor-roads for the nimble traffic of the present ...

Supported by facts and figures, the argument is impressive—until we bring other facts and figures against it. Every day forty thousand trains are travelling in Britain. Every year they carry a thousand million passengers, not to mention 289 million tons of freight and 72 million parcels.

Try to imagine the scene on a converted railway during the morning and evening rush-hours of a big city. A motorist might see something like it in a bad dream after driving to the coast on August Bank Holiday. We should still have a train of sorts—an endless line of motor vehicles so close together that they might much better be coupled and placed on rails.

The average regular passenger on a busy route, the commuter—

A man who shaves and takes a train
And then rides home to shave again

—has no idea of the total number of passengers on board. "Too many," he may feelingly say—but how many in round numbers? If his guess is "two or three hundred", the correct figure is probably at least seven hundred, or close to a thousand. Trains with loads like these come into the London stations every morning. Some are separated by minutes or seconds; some arrive together. Even busier is the evening traffic; for however keen the passengers are to be at work on time they are keener still to be home again.

When we are annoyed because a train is late, do we ever give a thought to all the work that lies behind this immense organization? Think of

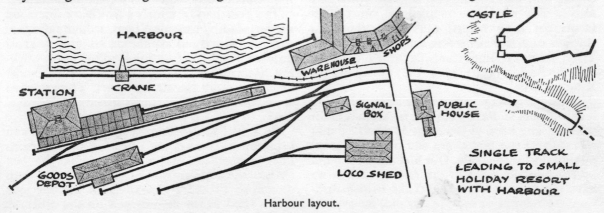

Harbour layout.

Waterloo with its twenty-one platforms and its daily total of about 1,600 separate train movements. The trains have to be brought in through a maze of tracks and then slipped out again for other trains to enter; and all this is done in the rush-hours at a speed which makes every second important.

Obviously, it would be over-ambitious of us to take a London terminal as the pattern for a station on our layout. A scale model of Waterloo would be the size of a tennis court. I also doubt if we have room on our baseboard for Grand Central Station or Pennsylvania Station in New York. These cathedrals of the railway are so vast that you could live in them, as people have in fact been able to do, for years on end without being detected. We could represent the actual structure quite acceptably, but it would be impossible to show the complexity of working: the train movements at Waterloo, for example, or the eighty tracks (in underground halls of solid rock) at Grand Central. For a reasonable pattern we must turn to something modest. Each of our terminal stations can serve a market-town or a small port, and the through-stations (one or two will be enough) can be tiny and quiet, like the halt on the moors where Richard Hannay stepped out to meet adventure. There is nothing more charming on any railway than a little country station, adorned perhaps with the stationmaster's roses and a tin advertisement for Mother Siegel's Soothing Syrup.

We shall not trouble greatly about platform lengths. If most model trains are longer than the platforms, so are many real trains—and not at small stations only. King's Cross passengers for Welwyn Garden City on a typical suburban train are given labelled carriages at the rear so that the other passengers can sit nearer the engine and find a platform outside when they alight. The problems created by short platforms (or long trains) are not confined to stations such as Knebworth and North Welwyn. They were an important factor in deciding British Railways to plan the rebuilding of King's Cross.

In the early stages of model railway planning it is sufficient to have a simple, rather makeshift station—any kind of home-made structure that will suggest the real thing and mark the stopping-point for the train. Our first aim is to build up the working basis of our railway. When we have done this we can begin, like British Railways, to rebuild or replace our old, inadequate

stations. Even then, the emphasis should be on the track arrangements rather than on the buildings, for the working facilities at a station govern the whole system and are themselves of great interest.

To take the same example of the North Hertfordshire line out of Kings' Cross, nothing complicated happens to a train for Hitchin once it has cleared the London terminus and is on its way. The train just goes. But at King's Cross various manoeuvres have been necessary. The train has been brought to the correct platform: the engine which hauled it there has been uncoupled at the buffer-stop; another engine has come from somewhere—perhaps from the sheds—and been attached to what is now the front; and the signals and turnouts have been operated to send the train out on its proper route at the proper time. Other operations will take place at Hitchin.

Similarly, the station on a developed model railway is not a mere stopping-place but a control-centre for the system. We may think of it as a brain; the open lengths of track are the nerves.

The design which we choose for a station area will depend upon the general working of the layout—above all, on the number of lines and the number of locomotives. As our first and simplest plan, we have a straight track running beside the single platform and ending in a buffer-stop. This is greatly improved by the addition of a siding, a turnout just in front of the station leading a short track along the side. With three items—buffer-stop, turnout and track unit—we have the basis of all station operations. However much our layout grows, however many locomotives we eventually run, the idea will be the same: to provide facilities for vehicle movements free of the main-line.

The principal formations which we discussed earlier—loops, reception lines, refuge sidings—can be varied and combined to give a great number of different station layouts. Loop working, for instance, is often better with a short extension from the straight part. The attached spur, the head-shunt, allows the engine to travel freely to and fro in shunting operations.

By using a turntable within a loop, we can bring an engine chimney-first on to the main-line, a problem that we studied in the last chapter. An extension of the loop in both directions provides a head-shunt on one side and a road to the engine-shed on the other. A turnout is not essential; without it we still have a useful, compact and good-looking station layout.

This arrangement is suitable for either a terminal or wayside station. Fundamentally the pattern is the same. Double-track, more engines and increasingly complex operations will lead to bigger terminals as we progress, but for the time being there will probably be little difference between the terminal sidings and those at the through-stations, except that the terminal sidings may incorporate one or two extra devices—crossovers, say, or a diamond.

Our first traffic is likely to be strictly passenger or strictly goods, the rolling stock being all of one kind. We shall not gnash our teeth about this. It is possible to have a single-traffic railway. As freight-only is commoner than passenger-only, we can confine our railway to freight services if the rolling stock is all wagons and vans. The train draws in at the main platform, and is free to use the sidings or any other facility—for the station, we may say, is designed for it. But what happens when the rolling stock is all carriages? Simple: we have an all-passenger railway! It operates on an island. After a bitter dispute between the railway company and the road-transport interests (it went on for years) the Island Council made an order limiting the railway to passenger traffic and the road services to goods. The regulation pacified both sides just at the time when they were threatening to withdraw from the territory, and the railway is now so popular with tourists that the directors are glad to be rid of freight (especially the guano and fish-manure).

The operator of an all-passenger line may be attracted by the idea of having one or two bays. These are formed of tracks and platforms behind the main area of the station. At some places the tracks lead straight in from the main running-road or from a branch line, and at other places they curve off like a siding. At each end of Cambridge Station, behind one of the longest platforms in England, is a fine example of a bay. Another type might equally well be called a side-platform, the area being open on one of its two sides.

Terminal bays are appropriate for a through-station as well as for a terminus. They can be developed from loops. A run-around at the back of the station is broken in the middle by a jutting platform which thus forms the buffer-stop end for each half. With Up and Down lines

and two platforms which face each other across the tracks—the commonest design for a through station the pattern can be doubled to give four bays, the equivalent of two broken loops, and some very pleasant working may be had by placing scissors crossovers between the main-lines and single cross-overs wherever they would be useful.

A different arrangement, the Rugby Plan, has the main-lines along the outside of the Up and Down platforms and the bays on the inside. They are then true bays—inlets separated at the centre by a square platform joining the Up and Down, as though the platform design for four outside bays had been turned around. A central road will be found useful for shunting and for storing vehicles clear of the running-lines.

Most through-stations have a plain layout not at all beyond the resources of the progressing beginner. With a couple of turnouts we can run a long loop from the mainline to the platform edge. For the second platform, when we have Up and Down lines, the design is repeated on the other side. Expresses sweep grandly by; other trains curve in on the loop to pick up passengers and drop them.

If the town is important enough for an occasional express to stop there, the platforms are built as islands between the main-lines and the loops. A still larger town would have a passing station with the main-lines alongside the

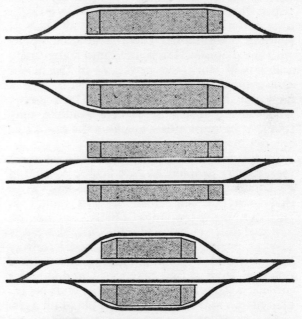

Simple through-station track diagrams.

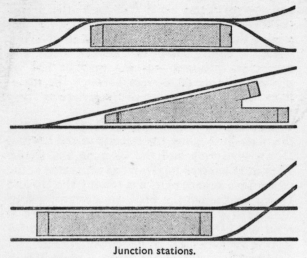

Junction stations.

platforms and a siding at the rear. The Up and Down lines could be connected by crossovers.

The problem of space, which confronts us always, is never felt more keenly than when we are designing a station layout. Seen in relation to the railway as a whole, the smallest addition is big enough to make us think and plan carefully before we introduce it. A new piece of track takes orders from the track already in position. A curve attached to the diverging arm of a turn-out must go where the arm tells it; and this may be well away from the area that we had in mind. The sweep of the curve takes us still further.

It is not at all difficult to plot a layout on paper. Neatly linked in a diagram, a few straight lines and a few curves will promise all kinds of running possibilities. There is nothing wrong with the diagram. Translate it into actual track and it will work out perfectly—in the model railwaymen's ideal home, a mansion with a habitable but unoccupied wing. The beginner who wants a reversing loop for example, may find that he must either abandon the project or enlarge his existing oval.

To progress in railway modelling we must regard every problem as a challenge. We should be continually encouraged by the knowledge that many of our difficulties are similar in pattern to those encountered in the construction of a real railway. If the plotting of track were as easy as peeling a banana, the model railway hobby would be less interesting and farther removed from actual practice. The difficulties provide a stimulus which keeps the craft perennially fresh and attractive to people of all ages.

The modeller at every stage is forced to use his ingenuity in economizing. Having quickly reached the point when he no longer dreams of an ever-spreading empire, he turns to schemes for enriching the area which he has already colonized. He wants as much variety and activity as are reasonably possible within a strictly defined space. How can a needed effect be achieved with the minimum of new track?

One of the pleasantest surprises in layout designing is the discovery of a better alternative to the plan which we originally considered. After a time certain formations lodge in our minds as stock ideas. Typical of these is the use of a crossover with a diamond crossing to link the inner of two main-lines with a siding. An ordinary turnout curves in to the outer main-line.

This formation is neat and compact. But a saving in space is not the only advantage that we may hope to secure when we look, as we always should, for a possible alternative method of doing what we intend to do. Very often indeed this intention concerns a re-arrangement of existing track. We want to create a new formation from the items which we already have. Can we, for example, produce the effect of a scissors crossing when we do not possess a diamond? We can; by placing two crossovers close together with their curves in opposite directions so that an engine on either track may pass through a facing turnout to the other.

The benefit is sometimes much greater than this. When four parallel lines of track, as at a siding, are connected with two others more or less at right angles to them, a couple of diamonds and four turnouts may be saved by first converting each pair of parallel tracks into a single track instead of leading all four separately into the double-line.

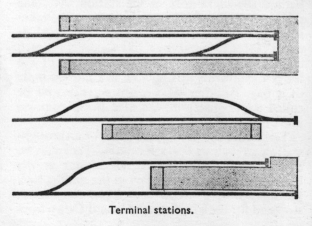

Terminal stations.

Above: Romney, Hythe and Dymchurch Railway (narrow gauge, 1 ft. 3 inches); 4-8-2 "Hercules."

Photographs by : J. F. Dobson, M. Mensing, R. F. Pulfer, Brian Western, Philip Kelley and D. Kelso.

Below : George Reffin's Denver and Santa Fé in TT.

Ladder sidings: the points lead in smoothly.

The possibility of linking two or more tracks before they reach the more important meeting-point is worth studying. It may be an improvement in itself or it may be combined with other improvements, to which it frequently points the way. Economy in running operations is no less important than economy in space and track. Indeed, it may be thought more important. Given unlimited room and a fortune to spend, we should still have to observe the common-sense practice of running the trains, as on a full-sized railway, with the minimum of fuss and the maximum of safety.

The placing of two crossovers together in a wavy formation is an old favourite among station layout designs. It creates a traffic route, excellent for engine release, across the track in the middle and at the same time links the middle track with the lines on the outside. The connection is complete, no diamonds are used, and the shunting can be carried out straight-forwardly.

Some arrangements are to be avoided simply because they happen to be wrong. One of the commonest errors occurs in the construction of ladder sidings. In diagram form these resemble the stepped pattern suggested by their name. But this pattern should be present only in the lay-outs of the straight parallel tracks and never at the edge where the curves lead into them. Many novices construct them like uncompleted loops, each a little further in than the one below it. They then have two ladders: one formed by the parallels, which is correct, and the other by the stepped effect at the edges, which is against actual practice. The curves should lead in directly and smoothly, as you see them in the diagram above.

A larger use of the double-into-single or single-into-double device may appeal to the beginner who is not yet operating two lines of main track. At a through-station the single main-line splits into a double loop, one side serving as the Up and the other as the Down. In the same way a single line at a terminus may be converted into a U, each arm of the U ending in a buffer-stop.

When the time comes for laying a second main-line, various alterations are usually necessary. It is therefore wise to keep the second track in mind from the outset, though not to the extent of hindering the immediate single line

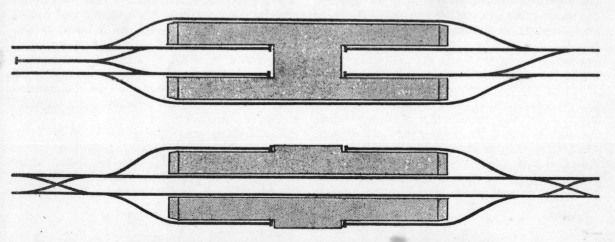

The Rugby station plan (above) and a through-station with terminal bays.

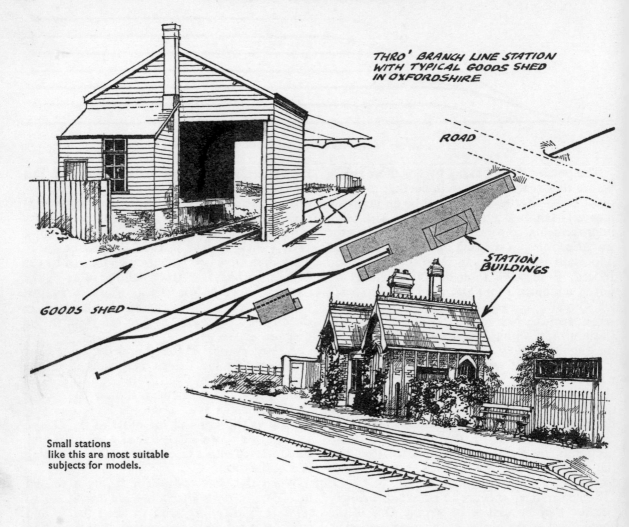

THRO' BRANCH LINE STATION
WITH TYPICAL GOODS SHED
IN OXFORDSHIRE

ROAD

STATION
BUILDINGS

GOODS SHED

Small stations
like this are most suitable
subjects for models.

plans. The branch-line too, should have a place in these considerations. After we have laid our main route double, we may want the same improvement on the branch. To bring a single track into a junction is easy, but when the two branch tracks have to join the two main tracks the Down of the branch must cross the main Up —normally by a diamond—to meet its sister line on the other side. Besides this complication, which is not large, we have the problem of fitting the new track into the general station design. A completely different plan may be forced upon us.

I shall have more to say later on this rather involved subject of stations and sidings. What I have already said points again to the import-

ance of showing a proper respect for simplicity. There is a sense in which a complex pattern can also be a simple one, plain, direct and economical in each of its parts. An eminent mathematician once told me that when he could approach a problem by a number of different ways he knew which of them was right. He drove through to his solution by the simplest route, which was also in terms of mathematics the most beautiful.

Could there be a better lesson for the designer of layouts? The plan which is essentially simple and geometrically pleasing—the plan which looks good on paper, clear and balanced and free of fussiness—is always the one to choose.

CHAPTER TWELVE

The Book of Rules

"WHEN two trains approach each other at a crossing they shall both come to a full stop, and neither shall start up again until the other is gone." This regulation is not Irish. It was issued in the Kansas of the rough, tough days and was the cause of some very heavy thought in the enginemen's shanties.

All railway systems operate according to various rules, some of them devised by the railways themselves and the others imposed from outside. During the last century, when the railways of Britain had grown into a network, nearly a hundred companies agreed to set up a central body which would bring their rules and charges into line, settle disputes, and generally enable them to work as a single unit. Since then the single system has become a fact. But the *Clearing House Rules and Regulations* is still one of the most carefully read books in Britain. It is a thick volume containing hundreds of numbered regulations and instructions. Railwaymen use it as a textbook for their examinations, and drivers, firemen and guards know large sections of it by heart.

To be acquainted with some of the official regulations is a help in railway modelling. A copy of those issued by the Ministry of Transport may be had for three shillings from Her Majesty's Stationary Office, Kingsway, London, W.C.2. We shall not send for it yet, but we may consider getting it later when our layout is closer in certain details to full-scale practice.

Meanwhile we will glance at a few of the rules that may interest us at our present stage. We find that facing points must be avoided as far as possible, that sidings should be laid out in such a way as to cause the minimum obstruction to passenger tracks, that station tracks should be arranged so as to prevent trains from standing on junctions at platforms, and that double lines must not end in a single line at a terminus. Stations should preferably not be built on gradients, and should have adequate street approaches (we must not forget footbridges where they are necessary) from high level, low level or track level. Similarly, a goods depot needs to be easily accessible, with a clear way in and out by rail and also of course by road.

Most of these rules are just what we would expect. They were dictated by commonsense, and the model railwayman will not go far wrong if he uses his own. All the traffic and layout rules for a station and siding resolve themselves into the one rule that minor movements should not interfere with major ones. Shunting operations should be free of the main-lines, and when this is not possible the shunting should be carried out speedily. With facing points at a sidings, there is a greater risk of accident as an engine or train may then back on to the main-line when another vehicle is approaching. The preference for trailing points, for working against the direction of main-line traffic, for placing the sidings on ground which slopes a little from the main-line, and for making the entrance to the sidings slightly indirect—all these are commonsense safety measures which the modeller may or may not be able to apply, according to circumstances. The distinction between facing and trailing points does not exist for the beginner who runs two-way traffic on a single line, and only the highly advanced modeller will think of arranging the siding on a gradient.

Safety points are another luxury for later days. The Ministry of Transport lays down that a pair must be provided at the main-line entrance to a goods siding. It also stipulates a minimum width of six feet for platforms at

 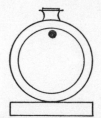 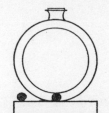 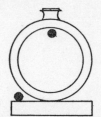 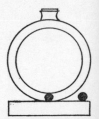

Express passenger, newspaper train or breakdown train.	Ordinary passenger, branch passenger or mixed train.	Perishable freight; parcels or empty coaching stock, at least half braked.	Express freight; at least a third with vacuum brakes.	Express freight, or perishable; at least four v.b. vehicles.

This is a simplified headlamps code.

small halts and of twelve feet for larger stations, but the modeller is wise not to trouble himself with dimensions which he cannot in any event reproduce at scale. While the veterans grumble that most miniature platforms are too short, many layouts would be improved by having them still shorter. If we are to be exact about scale, our model of a typical country station may take up a length of more than five feet. As this size is impossible on any ordinary layout, we had better ignore the official dimensions. When we are told, as we so often are, to "compromise" we need not choose a strictly mid-way position. We are equally unwise to attempt the dimensions which are *nearest* to what would be correct.

One of the worst trends in railway modelling arises from the notion that whatever would be much too big (or much too small) in correct scale must therefore be made as big (or as small) as possible. "I can't make the station six feet long", says the misled modeller, "but I can squeeze in four feet, which is pretty good". In fact, it may be pretty bad. The habit of regarding our railway as a picture will protect us from this error. Pictorial proportions and scale proportions are not the same and are frequently in opposition. What matters is the appearance of the whole. A station which is very long and supposedly "more" accurate (an impossibility, for a thing is either accurate or not) may be right out of balance with the rest, as well as the cause of ugly congestion.

While turntables must be as near as possible to the main-line, locomotive yards are required to be well away from it, for the sake of the passengers. This is less important when the engines are diesels and no one has to worry about smoke, ashes and coal dust.

Another rule says that all track must be fenced. Besides helping towards realism on a miniature railway, lineside fencing creates an impression of neatness. An area always looks more compact when it is marked off by a definite boundary. Placed close to a siding or yard, a length of wall will seem to draw the tracks into a tighter whole.

What a muddle confronts us in the area of any large station! Here are three empty wagons from North Wales with a covered china clay wagon from Cornwall. A van intended for the next station is sandwiched between two loads for a destination three hundred miles away. Two vans for Hull are in two different places. Alone on a loop, apparently forgotten, stands a forlorn passenger coach.

If we went behind the scenes, we should find the confusion to be that of a chess-board while a game is in progress. The vehicles which seem to be dotted about casually are all accounted for and have been moved into their positions according to a plan. On a wall of the control office is a map with pins that can be moved about, as at the headquarters of an army in action. Each pin carries a tab which completely identifies the vehicle whose position it marks. The tab for a train tells the controllers all that they want to know, including the names of the crew and the time for going on duty.

Train control was tried by the Midland Railway in 1908 and two years later was adopted by the Great Western with such success that it had become a normal part of railway operation long before British Railways introduced their modern system with the emphasis on centralized working. The control officers are concerned with the overall pattern along their own stretch of line. Their instructions, which may involve a large amount of detail, are then carried out according to the set rules.

Much of the final responsibility rests with the guard. A train in a marshalling yard is not made up in the way that happens to be easiest. The vehicles are assembled in a definite order to

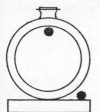 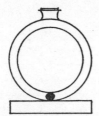  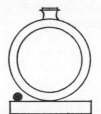 

| Express freight or livestock, not with continuous brake. | Light engine with not more than two brake vans. | Through freight not covered by other codes. | Mineral or empty wagon train—a code in every way simple. | Branch freight, pick-up, mineral or ballast train. |

"Freight" is the accepted railway term.

rules which are most often expressed in terms of what must *not* be done. Dangerous loads, such as oil or explosives, must not be placed next to the engine. Nor must loads of timber. Their position is at the rear, with the protruding ends, if the pieces are a little longer than the wagon, facing the direction of travel. When a long load of any kind is carried on two wagons, another flat wagon is placed in the middle even if it does not actually help to bear the load.

High loads must not be placed so near the rear brake-van that the guard is denied a clear view of the train. The latest guard-vans are fitted with periscopes. In America, where a freight train may stretch for more than a mile, the van has a caboose at the top where the guard sits and watches.

As far as possible, empty and loaded vehicles are not mixed. A long bogie wagon carrying a load must not come between other vehicles which are loaded. If all the other vehicles are empty, the bogie's place is either right behind the engine or right in front of the rear brake van.

Freight trains are "money trains" and the railways like them to have a load on the return journey. Empty wagons belong at the rear, in front of the brake-van. This is always the position for vehicles without continuous brakes, and so a mixed train in Britain will usually have the freight behind the passenger coaches.

Nearly everything seems to come at the rear! For a change, Pullman cars must be placed neither at the rear nor the front. They are placed within the body of the train but not next to six-wheeled or four-wheeled stock: a rule that will have to be ignored on many miniature railways. Six-wheeled and four-wheeled vehicles properly belong at either the back or front.

When there are two brake-vans, one of them will be at the head of the train. For most of our running, a single brake is sufficient. As the

trains will be short—four or five coaches are enough—the brake may not always be at the rear. In all longer trains it would be the last vehicle, or nearly the last. On a mail train full-length brake-vans are the sorting tenders.

A goods train occasionally includes a second engine which is not travelling under its own power. It immediately follows the live engine. Should the train be shunted, the dead engine is first uncoupled and stood off.

In the marshalling of a train which will stop at more than one station the order of vehicles corresponds, so far as the more important regulations permit, with the order of the stops. The vehicles for the first halt are placed at the head, behind the engine or the first brake-van. Those for the last halt are at the rear.

For better running on sharp curves the lighter vehicles should be towards the end of the train so that they are not pulled off the rails by heavier ones in front. I add this suggestion with the feeling that all our rules of working, taken together, are about as easy to obey as that perplexing regulation in Kansas! In practice, of course, we have to choose and adapt whenever two rules threaten to collide.

Naturally, the railways also have rules for loading and unloading. Sacks of light goods are arranged slopingly from end to end of the wagon with others lying flat in the angle of the V so that the load will not be thrown to and fro during shunting. Heavy sacks rest on end with another layer spread flat on top, parallel with the sides of the vehicle. Barrels are not carried on their ends, as we might suppose, but are roped together on their sides. The sides rest (or nest, as railwaymen say) on coils of rope.

Short lengths of timber, such as pit props, are loaded on end in high wagons and securely roped, or alternatively are laid flat at each end with others standing upright in the space between these two piles. Long timber girders and similar loads must be placed on the bolsters of the flat wagons in such a way that they can neither slip from the bolsters nor smash into the front or rear of the next vehicle.

The whole of a train, including the engine, is in charge of the guard. His name comes to him from the stage-coach days and has lost none of its meaning: he guards the train and all that it carries. His first duty on taking over is to make sure that the tail-lamps are in position and the couplings connected. There was a famous occasion on the Lynton and Barnstaple line—and it has probably occurred on other lines as well—when the passengers on an excursion trip were left behind. The uncoupled engine travelled from Chalfham to Barnstaple, the driver believing all the way that he had a happy party of excursionists behind him.

Lamps are important. The last vehicle of any train, however short, must carry a tail-lamp. We should have one in position whenever we are shunting, and we should also see that the headlamps are in place and correct for the train. Lamps may be bought or may be made at home by sticking a bead to a little circle of white cardboard.

As most of us know, headlamps are displayed in a code which identifies the type of train—as, for example, a single lamp high on the front of the engine to denote an ordinary passenger train, and one at top and bottom centre to indicate a through-freight. This is not the only code used on the railways. Another relates to the rolling stock. A six-wheeled truck is a Beaver, a bogie trolley wagon a Crocodile, an open truck an Open, a twin timber truck a Mite, a milk van a Siphon or a Lait, and a goods brake-van a Toad. To the wagon distributor, the mysterious message "Ohio one Coral" means "Send me quickly a wagon to carry glass".

We have all watched the manoeuvre known as loose-shunting. The wagons are loose from the engine which pushes them from one line to another and is then free to withdraw. When this is done with one set of vehicles we call it a single loose-shunt. In a double loose-shunt two sets are pushed, each through a different turnout on to another line—the sets being loose from each other as well as from the engine.

In fly-shunting the vehicles are uncoupled from the engine while they are in motion so that the engine and its load run on to separate tracks. This operation is not often seen on full-sized railways and is difficult to perform on a model layout.

A hump marshalling yard also lies beyond the scope of most of us. In this fascinating operation the shunting is done by gravity. The goods train is pushed into the sidings along a gradually rising track which descends much more steeply on the other side. As the vehicles pass over the hump they are uncoupled. They then run down the slope and fan out through various points, which have to be manipulated quickly, to the tracks intended for them. The work can be carried out at great speed with the use of radar-controlled braking.

A hump marshalling yard needs so much space on a real railway that it is most often found in open country. Model railwaymen who have room enough to install one may be helped in their experiments by the knowledge that a model vehicle with free-running wheels will coast down a gradient of 1 in 30.

At first the functions of freight, passenger and locomotive yards may be combined in one area. Whether we can have two sheds, for goods and engines, depends upon space. A small platform with a white railing round it will provide a cattle-pen for the goods yard and a simple shed-like building will serve as an office. For steam-type locomotives we should have an ash-pit, a coaling stage and a water tower. None of these, of course, will be used. It is sufficient to suggest the ashpit by painting a grey oblong on the baseboard or by sticking some real ash to a piece of card lightly coated with adhesive. The same idea can be adapted to provide a coal stage until we feel like attempting something more ambitious—and even then we shall not want much at a small station. While big yards may have a mechanical coaler, an engine at a little country station may refuel direct from a coal wagon. Nor do we need a water-softening plant. For the present at any rate, a water tower or two will be enough. If we prefer to make the tower, we can mount a suitably-sized tin, or the lower part of a round carton (how would a slice of Vim carton look?) on dowel rod.

Dowel is cheap and we should get a length from our handicraft shop. One of its many uses is in the construction of standpipes, a particularly important piece of equipment in the servicing of diesels. A diesel-electric shed usually has a pit between the rails and two floors or platforms above, one of them for working at axlebox level and the other at footplate level or a little higher. Everywhere are valves, pipes and coloured hoses, each colour indicating what the hose contains (green for fuel oil, yellow for compressed air) to make the connections easy and fool-proof. As everything is under cover, the modeller with diesels will be content with a shed. It should be long enough for two diesel units and may be built either as a run-through or as a dead-end.

Water is supplied from a standpipe. Another requirement which the diesel and the steam locomotive have in common is sand to provide a better grip on the rails whenever wheel-slipping may occur. A sand bin may be made of thick card with upright supports of balsa wood (a coal bin can be constructed in the same way) and the sand may be stuck to a packing of crumpled paper or to a cloth coated with shellac.

It is best, and correct, to place the various facilities in line so that an engine may pass from sand to coal, from coal to ashes, and then to water. A carriage yard for passenger stock may have a servicing platform with a coach-washer. Small pieces of leather or thick cloth, each with six sides, are pivoted on lengths of stiff wire fixed into dowels or, if the wire is stiff enough, rising straight from the baseboard. A coach passing under the wash-leathers rubs against them and causes them to revolve. If the apparatus is covered, the housing will be a shed without end walls.

A loading gauge should stand at the yard entrance; a crane will be ornamental and useful; and as all engines have to be lubricated, an empty corner may hold a shed for storing oil.

We can always conjure up something to fill a bare patch. By far the best idea is to visit a station yard, with official permission, or to inspect one from a convenient distance. The buildings, equipment and layout are then studied on the spot.

Some modellers find the construction and working of a goods yard of such fascination that they want nothing else. For them the train movements on a siding are like the moves in chess. After all, the distinction between a well-developed model railway and a well-developed model siding is not so great in operational terms as it may seem. The essential difference is that the railway includes the conception of definite journeys from Exe to Wye. While an engine may cover as much distance in the siding as it would in normal running on a limited layout, the average modeller prefers a full railway with the trains pulling out for the wide blue yonder.

The specialized layout may be combined with conventional working by attaching a long, narrow bench-type baseboard to the rectangle so as to provide a straight run on single or double track. To the specialist this run will be of secondary value. All that he asks is that the trains should go somewhere and come back again. It therefore satisfies him to have a rigged-up board with a loop at the far end or a remote-controlled turntable. Such a board may be erected on shelf-brackets or suspended, as from a picture-rail. I know of a model railroader in America who hoists his entire layout to the ceiling.

CHAPTER THIRTEEN

See How They Run!

WHAT would we say if we went to catch a train and found that it was composed entirely of open wagons? The earliest railway passengers travelled like coal. A few rode in carriages, but the carriages themselves were carried in the style of freight. They were horse vehicles owned by private individuals who had them loaded on to flat wagons and then climbed up to ride in the usual way.

It was not long before the pioneers realized that people, although always a nuisance, were a useful source of revenue. The Liverpool and Manchester Railway had carriages of a charming horse-coach pattern, and its passengers in the first month totalled ten thousand. But for many years the poor travelled hard; after being herded into open wagons, they were locked up in plain boxes without a window or a light.

Far from wanting everyone to be comfortable, the railway interests kept the cheapest accommodation crude and uninviting so that all but the poorest would pay the higher fares. "We do not feel disposed," wrote *The Railway Times*, "to attach much weight to the argument in favour of third-class carriages with seats." Prosperous-looking persons who travelled third were regarded with indignation, and the Manchester and Leeds Railway went so far as to hire sweeps who shook out their bags in the presence of these offenders.

What a change we see to-day! Our modern railways believe in comfort for all. Overcrowding of carriages is an annoyance, but the passenger unable to reach his handkerchief without standing, and unable to stand either, will agree that the compartment itself is extremely pleasant. Speed, comfort and convenience—these words sum up the passenger policy of the world's great railways. Every day when the Twentieth Century Limited leaves Grand Central Station a red carpet is rolled out; a gesture which may be said to symbolize the new attitude to the passenger.

The best-appointed trains and coaches of the last century were luxurious. Royalty, railway directors and rich members of the public travelled in palaces on wheels. Twice a year, with a pilot engine running fifteen minutes ahead, with platelayers posted all along the line, with all crossings guarded and all gates locked for two hours, Queen Victoria rode in high state to Scotland. Hardly less regal was the style of travel favoured by men like Andrew Carnegie, Henry Clay Frick, Jay Gould and the elder J. P. Morgan in the United States.

A suburban or branch-line train in Great Britain to-day may be composed of almost any kind of passenger vehicle except a Pullman. I often travel in suburban trains composed of corridor, non-corridor and open bus-like coaches. Some of the non-corridor vehicles are fairly new in appearance. Others look as though they had been borrowed in an emergency from a railway museum.

This mixing of stock is an advantage to the model railwayman. The expresses are composed of the larger or grander vehicles, and the less important trains of any other coaching stock in a combination that includes at least one brake van. The trains will not be long. For an express, six coaches will be a reasonable maximum and four quite enough. A suitable formation is a second-class coach, a dining car, and a first-class coach, with a brake-second or brake-composite at head and rear. As vehicles are dropped and picked up on the way, the formation may be different at the end of the journey. It would not be out of keeping for a big engine, such as a Pacific, to pull into its terminus with only two vehicles.

A composite coach (compo for short) is a

coach with two or more classes of accommodation. There are several different arrangements: first-and-second, first-brake, second-brake and first-second-brake. While the first-class passengers travelling a long distance will have complete coaches to themselves, those in suburban or local trains will more often share a coach with the second-class. The least common arrangement is the first-second-brake—two classes and a brake-van under the same roof.

An express in Britain may have fifteen coaches. It is seldom possible to use fifteen in a model train. We may eventually collect enough vehicles, but we shall not want the absurdity of a train whose engine arrives at one station while the brake-van is pulling out of the station just visited. The two coaches supplied in boxed sets by Hornby-Dublo, Tri-ang and Trix create, with their express locomotives, an agreeable impression of fast long-distance running. Most sets of this kind provide a first-second and brake-second coach. An ideal formation for a train of five coaches would be a brake-second, second, restaurant car, first, and brake-second again. Any main-line train may be of this pattern, with the difference that only an express would need the restaurant car. On other main-line journeys we might have a buffet car instead. The point is not important. An express may carry a buffet car (the Cambridge Buffet Express is well known) and a main-line train may also cover a long journey with neither buffet nor restaurant.

For a suburban train, a pleasant formation is brake-second, second, composite, and brake-second. It would be perfectly satisfactory to have only one brake. Hornby-Dublo and Tri-ang offer a number of suburban coaches in standard British Railways livery and in Southern Region green. A couple of Trix suburban coaches look well behind a 4-4-0 Hunt Class engine of the Eastern Region.

Best of all for the beginner is the local or branch-line train with its many acceptable variations. Country working permits more freedom than any other: short trains, mixed trains, and any of the smaller types of engine. A local may be run with only two coaches and it is not departing from actual procedure to place the engine between them. The diagramming for a branch-line depends upon the importance of the branch and the kind of journey. Does the line run to a large town which made the mistake of disliking railways when they were new? Is it a place which was a village in the time of Stephenson or Brunel and is now big and booming because of a local industry? Such a town may be served by fast trains like those on the main route. Again, it may be a small quiet town with a typical country service. We can sometimes make much the same kind of trip in a suburban train when it is ten or twenty miles from the city. A suburban frequently sets off as a fast train, stops at an important town, and then takes on the character of a country local.

On the average branch-line two non-corridor brake-composites would agree with Western Region (Great Western) practice. A brake-second and a composite fit the North Eastern (L.N.E.R.) and London Midland (L.M.S.) procedure.

We must not forget the specials—holiday trains, boat trains, and others, both passenger and freight. They should be short. Cows are milked twice a day, and we do not want five or six milk vehicles to be tied up for long intervals. A milk train calling at a dairy factory will include a tank wagon. For ordinary country stops, vans and churns are more in keeping. Both methods of collection can be used together, and the same train may have a utility van in addition to the customary brake.

Boat trains are delightfully comfortable. First-class accommodation is essential and we should, if possible, have a Pullman. Here is the opportunity to use an Ocean Mails coach, if our railway represents the practice of B.R. Western Region. Baggage vans are vital; there is always a great quantity of luggage on a train which is carrying people to or from a ship.

The Pullman Special contrasts with the crowded excursion train. For parties and cheap day trips the coaching stock will be mixed. The big holiday trains will have first-class accommodation, dining or buffet cars, and an express-type engine. I suggest a maximum of five coaches, one of them first-class.

Passenger coaches may properly be placed in a newspaper train. As two parcel vans, a passenger coach and a brake-van will make a balanced set, this special is another which needs nothing unusual. Like the milk train, it runs at wide intervals. The parcel vans may be incorporated in ordinary passenger trains, ordinary mail trains, and the Post Office train, a unit which is highly special.

Far from being a fairly modern innovation, the travelling post office is nearly as old as the railways. The idea of sorting the letters in transit was put forward by Frederick Karstadt, son of a Post Office surveyor, and by the summer of 1838 a train on the Grand Junction line was collecting and dropping sorted mail on the run between London and Bletchley. As the train passed through a station, a net grabbed the waiting load. While this is still the method for collecting, the pouches to be dropped are no longer thrown out of the window; they are whipped from the traductor arms on the coach by a lineside net, and so a double snatch takes place.

Not all mail trains are travelling post offices, and not all T.P.O.s are fitted with receiving and despatching apparatus. We can run a Limited Mail like an ordinary passenger train, and if we have an Ocean Mails coach we may use it for G.W.R. work. There are many vehicles which can be incorporated in passenger trains—vans for fish, fruit, milk and parcels, and various wagons. Anything which might normally be marshalled in a passenger train (except, of course a freight vehicle in a passenger and freight assembly) is known as coaching stock. To this category belong vehicles as varied as the dining car and the pigeon van. The utility van and the furniture wagon are coaching stock no less than the parcel van, the mail van, and the guard's brake-van with its luggage.

All items of rolling stock which do not fit the simple description of coach, wagon or van are known as special vehicles. At least one of them, the petrol tank van, appears on most model railways in the early stages of development. Equally familiar is the cable-drum wagon.

The travelling breakdown crane attached to a locomotive and brake-van makes a special train whose claim to that title no one will dispute. Accidents occur on the best-regulated model railways, but they tend to become remarkably frequent as soon as a Big Hook has been acquired. It is advisable not to stage a catastrophe; too often repeated it may lead to a real one.

In nothing is the model railwaymen better served than in the supply of special vehicles. Hornby-Dublo, Tri-ang and Trix in Britain, Märklin, Rivarossi and Pocher on the Continent, Lionel, Mantua and Varney in the United States: taken together the lists issued by these manufacturers contain almost every special vehicle that would be found on a real railway, except Swedish coaches for mothers and children and the travelling dental-clinics for Australians with toothache.

There is a similar richness in the general rolling stock and especially in the freight. No one who compares the newest catalogues with earlier ones can fail to note a number of changes, all testifying to the prosperity of railway modelling. The hobby is now resolutely up-to-date. In addition to providing enough traditional vehicles to fill most of the gaps which existed before the war, the leading makers have turned out, often with great ingenuity, stock of a kind which formerly was unknown to model railways and real railways alike. As diesel-electric vehicles have come to British Railways, so have they appeared in the lists of Tri-ang, Trix and Hornby-Dublo. The adoption of overhead power systems, with pantographs collecting the current from catenaries suspended above the track, is Tri-ang's and Trix's latest response to modernization. Similarly, we are witnessing the introduction of freight stock which reflects, sometimes remarkably, certain aspects of the modern age. Tri-ang has a rocket-launching wagon and Lionel an atomic energy disposal car for removing the hot particles given off in nuclear fission. The world of model railways is changing fast.

We see, too, a growing internationalism. What is said of engineers, that they do not recognize frontiers, may equally be said of those who engage in any form of model engineering. Travelling across the world, the magazines of the movement foster an interest which grows steadily stronger and is now being expressed, to a greater degree than ever before, in an exchange of rolling stock. Continental models

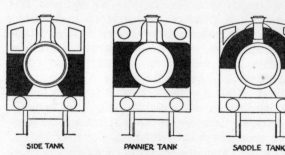

SIDE TANK   PANNIER TANK   SADDLE TANK

run in Britain, and British models in Europe and America. Trix has a range of American-style stock, including a Texaco tank car and a caboose, and Rivarossi pays full tribute to such lines as the Pennsylvania, Reading, Milwaukee, Boston and Maine, Michigan Central, Illinois Central, Great Northern, Union Pacific, Southern Pacific and Santa Fe.

Märklin produces Swiss and Dutch vehicles as well as those of the German Federal Railways. In England Tri-ang offers Vista-Dome cars, observation cars with end-windows, baggage cars, a pickle car, a snow-plough, a caboose and various other vehicles, all designed to be hauled by the Tri-ang transcontinental diesel locomotives. There is also a Tri-ang Pacific engine, with an eight wheel tender, for those who are loyal to the representation of steam-power.

The enthusiast need not rely on the proprietary systems. He may have his locomotives built to order by a model engineering firm at about three times the price of a similar ready-made model (depending on the type of motor, the amount of detail, and the time allowed to the builder) or he may build his own, with help in the form of parts and plans. Boilers, wheels and other parts may be bought separately from various sources. This method reaches back to the last century and the early days of *Model Engineer*. The newer method uses kits: casting kits for screwdriver assembly, kits of metal sheets for soldering, and even cheap kits of polystyrene mouldings. Most American engines can be constructed from castings in Mazak, an alloy of zinc and lead.

The skilled, patient and determined modeller may prefer to construct everything from scratch. This is the hard way and is not for the beginner. Now and then we see a masterpiece which was produced at the first attempt; what we do not see are the total failures gathering dust and cobwebs in the back corners of boot-cupboards. The best course for the average beginner is to buy a ready-made engine—his second if he has begun with a boxed set—and to construct a wagon or van from time to time with kits from Peco, Gem, Hamblings, Bradshaw, K's, CCW Productions or any of the other makers who advertise in the model railway magazines. Peco's respect for realism extends to the under-frames of its vehicles. It even goes a little further, for two of its coal-wagons are made to look coal-smeared and worn.

Of the ready-made locomotives I need say nothing here, for the beginner is either acquainted with them already or is able to study them in the catalogues, nearly all of which reproduce the actual colours. I have left the locomotives until last because they tend to bulk too large in the eye of the beginner. As the source of haulage power they are naturally the most important and most interesting vehicles on any railway, actual or miniature. But they are still only a part of the whole; and it is as a whole, with every piece performing its appointed duty, that a model railway should be conceived, built and operated.

Too often the young modeller thinks of the train as "something for the engine to pull". Knowing this, I have tried to show the importance of the passenger and freight vehicles and the broad pattern of their working. The business of a railway is to run trains and not to exercise its engines, which are there because of the trains and for no other reason. An express train is composed of superior stock and is automatically given the right-of-way, together with any other priorities that will help to speed it on the journey; but none of these privileges exists for the flattery of the handsome engine at the front!

Handsome it is. Of all machines that travel on land the kingliest is the big steam-engine, sweeping along in the easy confidence of its power or breasting a hill in rugged majesty. Yet a popularity poll might well give first place to the humble tank. A Pacific or a Britannia receives our admiration; a little engine, plodding in the yards or setting off gallantly with the local, is sure of our affection.

On any layout the tank has a great number of duties. This is true also of the full-scale railways, as every loco-spotter knows if he frequents a station area. Besides chugging in the yards, the tank may haul the pick-up goods and sometimes a more important train over a much longer distance.

The Tri-ang saddle-tanks, electric and clockwork, are a reminder that these engines, which we associate first with the Western Region, were once in great use on the railways of Britain. When engines were small, the tank fitted conveniently over the boiler like a saddle; but as the boilers continued to grow the tank was given a different shape. By making this alteration the Great Western developed the saddle-tank into the pannier tank which has a flat top suggesting the panniers, or baskets, carried on an animal. Water is needed at fairly frequent intervals.

While I can understand that the model railwayman of to-day may like to have a diesel shunter, the enthusiast for modern efficiency will perhaps confess to a feeling of loss when the last little nameless tank moves out of the yards, never to return.

CHAPTER FOURTEEN

Guardian Arms

SIGNALMEN on the early railways did not have to pull levers or press buttons; they were themselves the signals. Like policemen on traffic duty in the streets, they stood at intersections and gave their orders with motions of the arm.

There were, too, signalmen who rode with the drivers. When London underground trains going in opposite directions from Baker Street and Swiss Cottage (now stations on the Inner Circle) could pass only at St John's Wood, which had a double line and crossing facilities, a signalman with a blue belt travelled on one engine and a signalman with a red belt on the other. Neither of them was allowed to take the train beyond St John's Wood. Before the trains could proceed under signalman's authority, blue-belt and red-belt therefore had to change places. This they did with such skill that people went to St John's Wood station for the free entertainment of watching two men leap from two engines, rather like escaping train-bandits, and slide along the platform for twenty-five feet.

Far more entertaining, or alarming, was a scene occasionally witnessed on the pioneer railways of America. So that trains could pass each other on a single-track route, spurs were led away from the track at intervals. A marker indicated the midway point between one refuge and the next. When two trains were running towards each other head-on, the train which had passed the marker could rightly continue while the other had to reverse, pass through the turnout, and wait on the spur. It was an admirable arrangement except that it failed to allow for the possibility that two trains might reach the midway point more or less together. When this happened, the meeting began with an argument and sometimes ended in a fight which might easily become a free-for-all, the train crews having the violent support of the passengers.

Drivers also used to race each other to the spurs and intersections. "What a way to run a railroad!" is a saying, applied now to hopeless inefficiency in any form, which had its origin in the sudden meeting of two trains on a single-track line. One day an American farmer was ploughing a field when he saw a west-bound express and an east-bound freight rushing towards each other. Asked later what he had done about it, he replied: "Not a thing, I just thought to myself, 'What a heck of a way to run a railroad!'"

Signalling made the railways much less dangerous, though for a long time they were still far from safe. Few Americans to-day, when they sip an iced highball, connect the drink in a tall glass with the hoisted ball which was the first American railway signal. Suspended from a kind of lofty gallows on the Newcastle and Frenchtown line in Delaware, it signified All Clear Ahead.

This hoisting of a visible sign was greatly superior to the system used in Britain once the human signalling arm had been replaced by a mechanical one. The early history of the semaphore, which was introduced in 1840, provides a classic example of cleverness without commonsense, for the ingenuity shown in the actual control of the signals was spoilt by the error of indicating Line Clear negatively, as a complete blank. The arm dropped and disappeared from view. To make sure that it would not be visible to the driver, a slot was cut in the upright post.

Signals were still built with these slots, even in posts of latticed iron, eighty years after the disappearing arm had disappeared for good. Railways have always been a curious mixture of the conservative and the progressive, and no-

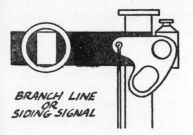

BRANCH LINE
OR
SIDING SIGNAL

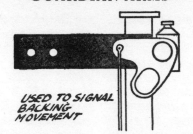

USED TO SIGNAL
BACKING
MOVEMENT

MOVE FORWARD
FOR SHUNTING

where is the mixture stranger than in the story of signalling and safety. Some railways were backward in one aspect and some in another; and the rest were backward in everything until an Act of 1889 demanded the use of block signals, the interlocking of signals and points, and the provision of continuous brakes on passenger vehicles, thus compelling all the lines to adopt measures whose worth had long been proved.

British Railways are now reaching the standard set by the old Great Western with its automatic train control. In this system a shoe underneath the engine comes into contact with a ramp between the rails. If the distant signal is at Clear the ramp is electrified and the current picked up by the shoe rings a bell in the cab. This does not mean that the driver hears nothing at other times; on the contrary, a Caution signal sounds an emphatic horn in the cab and gradually applies the brakes. Can we laugh at Edward Bury who, as far back as 1840, devised for the London and Birmingham routes a cab signalling device which blew the whistle and shone a red lamp in the driver's face?

The greatest of all the contributions to safety came from George Westinghouse, a boy soldier in the American Civil War who was still little more than a boy when he invented the compressed-air brake. Speeds were increasing in the eighteen-sixties, and they have continued to increase. No matter what improvements are brought about in braking, the hardest part of

driving a train must always be the stopping. The modern problem of halting a tremendously fast train is essentially not different from the pioneer's problem of safely halting a slow train when brakes were primitive.

Because the ambling trains of 1841 could not always stop in time, the distant signal was introduced to warn the driver in advance. Six years later the Great Northern fitted this signal all along its main line.

A Distant in the On position tells the driver to go ahead with caution and be prepared to stop if the next home signal is against him, as it will be unless something has happened during the interval—such as the switching of an oncoming train into a loop. The arm is distinguished by a vee notch at the end and a black vee stripe on both sides, with a yellow background facing the driver and a white background showing in the opposite direction. At night a yellow light shines for On and a green light for Off.

Interlocking ensures that the distant signal agrees with the home signal to which it refers; it can be moved to the clear position only when the signal for stopping is also cleared. The distant may be three-quarters of a mile, or a little less, from the box controlling it, but so much depends upon the gradients and other factors that there can be no strict rule beyond the obvious requirement that the cautioned driver has a chance to act.

In some circumstances the Distant and Home

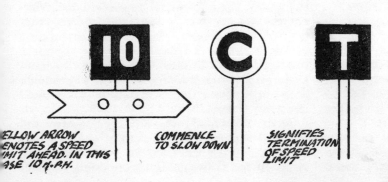

YELLOW ARROW
DENOTES A SPEED
LIMIT AHEAD. IN THIS
CASE 10 M.P.H.

COMMENCE
TO SLOW DOWN

SIGNIFIES
TERMINATION
OF SPEED
LIMIT

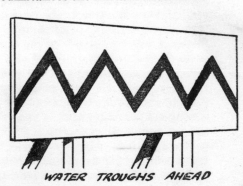

WATER TROUGHS AHEAD

share the same post, with the Home at the top. This combination of different and independent signals is extremely attractive on a model railway though it may not be convenient to operate the two from separate boxes—one from the local box and the other from the box ahead.

The Home or Stop signal is red on the driver's side and has a white vertical stripe near the straight outer edge, in the same position as the painted vee on the Distant. We may see the same design on the back, but here the vertical stripe is black and the background white. The spectacles through which the light shows are red and green, the red as everyone knows being in front of the light when the signal is at Danger.

Home signals stand at the entrances to block sections and at turnouts. A train running on a long stretch where there are no points at all will be signalled at intervals if the road is required to be clear for a block ahead. At a turnout the Home signals have much the same function as signposts in that they show the driver the road

ing the block ahead, tells the driver to proceed with extreme caution; the calling-on, or draw-ahead, warns him to go no further than the line is clear when he draws forward (perhaps for water) within station limits; and the shunt-ahead, which may be a dwarf semaphore or a ground disc, gives him shunting instructions. He may sometimes pass a stop signal when his duty is shunting only.

Subsidiary signals are seldom found on a model layout, but we may have any or all of the others—home, distant and starter. Wherever possible they stand to the left (right on G.W.R.) with the arm pointing away from the road which it controls. In single-line working the arms may face both ways on the same post, for Up and Down.

Correct procedure demands so many signals that a small miniature line may easily become cluttered with posts and arms. It is much better to simplify. Signals may be confined to points where there is a choice of route and to station

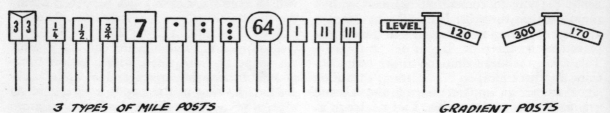

3 TYPES OF MILE POSTS   GRADIENT POSTS

which he is about to take. The main support of this junction or splitting signal is usually shaped like a T with a shorter post at each end of the horizontal piece. If one road is more important than the other, the signal arm controlling it will be higher than the other arm; which in practice often means that the top arm refers to the straight-on road. When a good many ways diverge the arms are grouped on short posts (*dolls* to the railwaymen) supported by a girder bridge, the familiar gantry. As with the simpler splitting signal, the arms or posts are of different heights according to the priority of route.

A starter signal is most commonly seen at the forward, or engine-end, of the station platform where it controls the starting of a train into the advance section, ahead of the box, and permits the signalman to take care of shunting and general station duties without having to ask the box ahead for acceptance. The arm is like that of an ordinary home signal.

Besides these running signals, the railways use a number of subsidiary ones. The calling-off signal, placed below the stop signal protect-

ends, where a starter increases the impression of careful working.

There is little practical value nowadays in making our signals from bits and pieces. Various excellent kits are obtainable from Hamblings, Scalesig and other manufacturers, while those who prefer the ready-made article are sure to find what they want. Gem and S & B Productions have realistic signals priced at less than three shillings.

Boxes, levers, frames, wires and motors may all be bought. The old style of mechanical operation loses its worst terrors in the Mer-control system which runs the control wire through thin copper tubes so that the sliding action is kept free from the lineside supports. Enterprisingly, Tri-ang provides a solenoid assembly which allows the beginner to graduate with ease from hand-operation to remote electrical control.

At the crossroads where the policeman used to stand we now have, in most of our towns, a set of lights for Caution, Stop and Go. Similarly, on the railways, lights are doing some of the work once undertaken by the signalling policemen, at first with their own arms and later with wooden ones which they operated on the spot.

The first colour-light signals in the United Kingdom were fitted on the Liverpool Overhead Railway as long ago as 1920. Since the war the Docker's Umbrella, like the New York El, has disappeared (I travelled three hundred miles to ride on it before the end) but its signalling system is coming into ever-wider use and is already as familiar on miniature railways as on the full-sized ones. Hornby-Dublo's colour-light signals are of the two-aspect type, as were the Overhead's, and are produced in three patterns, home, distant and junction. Trix, Märklin and Rivarossi offer automatic control from the track.

As I have briefly explained, automatic train control operates on the engine itself, and block-signalling means that a section of track (doubled for the Royal Train) is always clear ahead. In automatic power-signalling the train passes over an electrical treadle which works the signals immediately behind and in front but does not brake the train.

On most model layouts a form of block-working exists already in the sense that only one train, except in Trix, can run on the same length of rail. Track-circuiting is possible, as Ernest F. Carter describes in *Model Railway Power Signalling* (Percival Marshall) but is not much favoured by the beginner, who may properly regard it as a luxury.

Mechanical methods are sometimes the subject of experiment by very young beginners who hope to make the engine strike a trigger as it passes. This idea has better possibilities in O gauge than in OO and I once employed it with fair success on a clockwork layout. But it tends to be cumbersome and to look out-of-place even when it proves successful—and more often than not the experiment ends in frustration and a dismal tangle of wire.

With the electrical method, which is altogether neater and more promising, we are completely free from the problem of arranging a lever so that the engine will hit it forcefully and yet not be derailed, at the same time letting it jump back again for the next operation. The train on an electrical track-circuit is not asked to strike anything; it works the control simply by being there.

Two wires connect the signal with a section of track. One leads to an ordinary continuous running-rail and the other to a rail which is cut off electrically from its neighbours, by having gaps sawn at the ends if the railway is electric, and by further insulation if the sleepers are of metal as they may be on a clockwork layout. The desired condition is that the broken rail should be dead except when an engine comes along and completes the circuit by forming a metal bridge. A current then passes through the solenoid of the signal, either from the running circuit or from a separate one. A separate one is preferred.

The system may be applied to three-rail electrical operation where only two of the rails carry the traction current for the train, to clockwork and steam railways whose tracks do not of course supply power to the engines, and to stud-contact layouts. Regrettably, the railway which might use it most is the one for which it is un-

suited. A gap in a length of two-rail electric track makes normal running impossible as both rails belong to the circuit that drives the trains.

There are few problems in railway modelling which have not been solved, sometimes by a large number of enthusiasts and sometimes by a lone pioneer here and there. But the solution is seldom one for the novice. The owner of a two-rail electrical layout may console himself that automatic signalling is less of a pleasure in the end than straightforward operation from the cabin. This may sound like sour grapes, but we can in fact make our railway automatic to the point where interest fades.

A refinement that we may attempt with success is the interlocking of signals and points. Joining the two by purely mechanical means may present various difficulties, and many will be happier with an electrical method. Some power-signals are worked by a pair of solenoids, one pulling the arm down and the other pushing it up, while a second type has a single solenoid to pull the arm and a counterweight to move it into the Danger position. The double action requires the switching on of the current at the moment of operation. In this it differs completely from the solenoid - counterweight arrangement which uses a constant flow while the signal is at Clear, the breaking of the current restoring the arm to Danger. The interlocking method to be employed therefore depends upon the manner of control. With the single solenoid it may be convenient to break-and-make the circuit at the lineside in the same movement that changes the points. The alternative is lever operation at the box. Here, too, we have a choice. One lever can be fixed to throw the points and the signal arm together, or two levers can be arranged in such a way that the points and signal which they separately operate are bound to agree.

As these techniques belong to a later phase in our progress, I will not describe them here in the detail that their construction demands. Signalling is full of intricacies and for that reason is deeply fascinating. My rough outline may suggest the possibilities that wait to be explored by the modeller who, having given the shape of unity to his layout, is keen to introduce further and more ingenious improvements.

Meanwhile we can study the signalling arrangements at our local station. If we stand near to a signal box we shall hear the signalmen conversing in bell code: perhaps the four even beats for *Is line clear?* and then the two beats for *Train entering section*. The signalman acknowledges each message by repeating it to the sender. He "accepts" the train which is "offered", warns the box in front, and transmits *Train out of section*, two beats followed by a pause and a single beat, when the train has passed or, as he would say, is no longer "on line".

If we want this system on our layout we can use a doorbell. The drawback is that other people in the room may be less keen than ourselves on an arrangement which produces a frequent ringing. Even a station bell, giving one beat for a train approaching No. 1 Platform and two beats for a train coming in at No. 2, may be a little too much for the family's nerves. The place for the bell system is a loft or shed where parents will not be roused to wrath against the misguided people who write books about railway modelling.

Two Belgian locomotives, Type S. Pacific (*above*) and Type 42 Atlantic.

Without rivals on the rails, what might the steam locomotive have become?

(*Belgian Railways*)

The lone engine: a cutting in Germany.

Steam and snow.

Evening halt in the Black Forest.

Majesty. (*German Federal Railways*)

One of the Benelux trains.　(*Belgian Railways*)

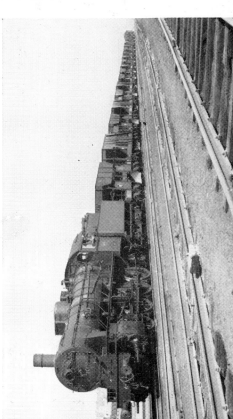

... retains its kingliness—even when hauling a mineral train.　(*Belgian Railways*)

Electric train leaving Lille.　(*French Railways*)

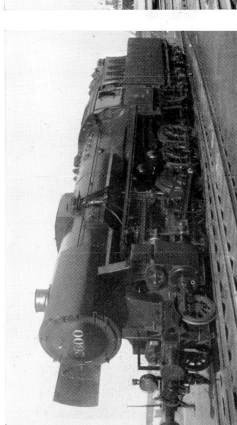

For all the modernization of European railways, the steam engine retains its kingliness—even when hauling a mineral train.

In contrast: Gare Verviers Central   (*Belgian Railways*)

Wavre St. Catherine.   (*Belgian Railways*)

Station buffet at Poitiers.   (*French Railways*)

Contrasts in modern station architecture—Blankenberge and ...

Clean, airy, modern. The station at Poitiers.   (French Railways)

Paris-Lyon—a familiar scene everywhere when suburban trains arrive.
(French Railways)

Night train at Lille.   (French Railways)

Terminus Rome   (E.N.I.T.)

Semaphore with automatic colour-light signals. *(French Railways)*

Outside Paris-Lyon *(French Railways)*

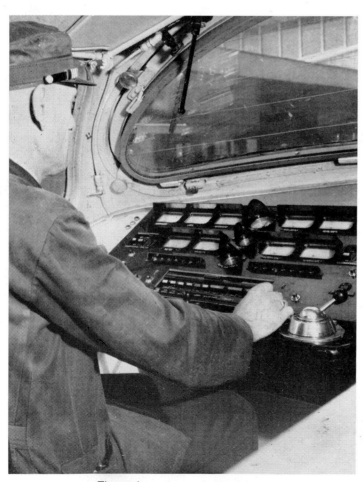

The modern way—an Italian driver *(E.N.I.T.)*

Between Paris and Lille.

Signal box at Paris-Nord. 319 buttons control 102 sets of points and 493 routes. *(French Railways)*

A locomotive of this class travelled at 205 m.p.h.   (*French Railways*)

Santa Fe men lever a welded rail into position
(*Santa Fe*)

This is a railway station—at Heidelberg.   (*German State Railways*)

Catenaries and cloud.   (*French Railways*)

French radio-controlled train.
(*French Railways*)

Cajon Pass, California.

(Santa Fe)

CHAPTER FIFTEEN

Scales and Rails

WHEN the Paddington-Penzance Cornishman steamed out of London at ten-fifteen on the morning of 20 May, 1892 the running rails along the route were seven feet apart. At four o'clock the following morning the same train, having left Penzance on another journey, rolled into Swindon on a track which was still seven feet wide. This may seem like saying that the sun went down in the west, except that twenty-four hours later the night mail from Paddington travelled down to Penzance on rails which were narrower by more than two feet.

Almost overnight the long and bitter Battle of the Gauges had ended, at least, in Britain. It still flares up here and there when railway lovers speak of the Great Western and of Isambard Kingdom Brunel. There are some who approve of Brunel's seven-foot gauge entirely and others who say, quoting Brunel himself, that it should have been bigger still; while the anti-Brunel party contends that it was plain foolishness to introduce a gauge which differed at all from the one already adopted on two thousand miles of railway in the United Kingdom.

Such was the bitterness of the rivalry that the narrow-gaugers descended to the knavery of putting hot water in a narrow-gauge tender and sand in some of the Great Western axle-boxes. So far as I know, the history of the miniature gauges, close though it is to the history of gauges at full-scale, contains nothing of this kind!

I doubt if the old controversy will be settled by pointing out that track-gauge itself is less important than loading-gauge, the height and width of the vehicles. Brunel's rolling stock was not very much wider than the rolling stock on rails 4 ft. 8½ in. apart. In South Africa a track-width of only 3 ft. 6 in. accommodates engines which would be too big for Britain. Most puzzling of all to many is the discovery that the enormous locomotives of North America run on the same width of track as the smallest tank meandering on a branch-line through the English countryside.

A time came in the history of model railways when they too were in need of standards. The movement towards greater uniformity gained its first momentum in the United States where the hobby can be traced back to 1904. So much interest was created in the early 1930s by the model trains at two great Century of Progress exhibitions that in 1935 about seventy model railroad clubs met in Milwaukee to discuss their common future. The National Model Railway Association, which was the fruit of that meeting, quickly grew into a thriving society with its own magazines, bulletins, conferences and exhibitions and a membership that was worldwide. Its main problems were those of scale and gauge. Despite all the different ideas (there are as many perfect gauges as there are modellers) the second meeting four years later agreed on certain standards.

Four years later was 1939. Model railwaymen in Britain had followed with approval the activities of the N.M.R.A., for the problems on both sides of the Atlantic were essentially the same. British equipment had come to be made in at least fifteen different sizes. In the eyes of advanced modellers the manufacturers were like so many Brunels. But the outbreak of war put an end for the time being to the production of modelling goods, and there seemed no reason why, if all the makers had to stop, they should not agree to various standards before they all began again. The modellers saw their chance and took it.

Meeting in 1941 under the chairmanship of

J. N. Maskelyne (then Editor, and now Consulting Editor, of *Model Railway News*), representatives of the clubs and of the manufacturers and the model railway press set up a body whose aims are explained by its title, the British Railway Modelling Standards Bureau. The standards sought were principally of gauge and scale.

Gauge is the distance between the inner edges of the rails (measured at $\frac{5}{8}$ in. from the top in real practice) and scale is the ratio in size of the model to the thing modelled—often called the prototype, though the prototype of a model would strictly be a model itself. These definitions are so simple that they hardly need mentioning, but to understand the broad idea is by no means the same as understanding the details.

With all proportions the same, we should be able to know the gauge from the scale or the scale from the gauge. But scaling is a curious process which seldom works out exactly as we might expect. A model which looks a perfect picture of the real thing may differ from it in performance. Too high a degree of realism may produce a low degree of practical efficiency, and the engine which delights us in a glass case would probably be outshone on the steam track by a more rugged model.

In modelling, as in other fields of life, the ideal and the practical are forever challenging each other. We want the model to be a perfect reproduction and we also want it to work perfectly. When these two requirements conflict most of us insist on the practical without losing our respect for the precise. So small is the difference between the two—a millimetre here and half a millimetre there—that the beginner, especially if he has a proprietary train set, may disregard it in his own working. What he cannot ignore so easily is the effect which the pursuit of exact measurements has had on the adoption of scales and on the technical language which railway modelling employs. In reading the magazines and catalogues of the hobby, and in talking with advanced modellers, it will help him to know how the scales and gauges compare and what is meant by such terms as fine scale and coarse. All these distinctions are best understood by tracing their development and discovering why they exist.

At the beginning of the century the small size was Gauge 1. While this gauge still has its enthusiasts, the other gauges of that period are now too large for the average indoor modeller. Gauge 2 appeals only to a few veterans and Gauge 3 has moved outdoors to the steam track where everything is bigger.

By the beginning of the First World War, some modellers were working in a smaller gauge of seven millimetres. As it came next below One it should logically have been Nought, but the zero was changed into a letter of the alphabet.

A new size appeared soon after the 1914 war. As it was half as big as the next smallest (three and a half millimetres compared with seven) the manufacturers dubbed it HO, for Half-O. W. J. Bassett-Lowke, Trix and Bonds O' Euston Road pioneered HO with the journalistic support of Henry Greenly who had designed it. For clockwork engines the track width was excellent. But a second change occurred at about the same time. Electrically-driven engines were becoming more popular and the makers had difficulty in building a model that would be tiny enough for the gauge and yet powerful enough to satisfy the modeller.

Hard though it is to believe, an extra half a millimetre—about a fiftieth of an inch—was all that the makers needed to pack in the extra power. To get the additional space they constructed a new scale.

Up to this point, scale and gauge had been the same. But now the operator could run a locomotive of the new 4 mm. scale on track of the old HO gauge; or he could keep to the HO dimensions for track and rolling stock alike. The gauge itself no longer defined the scale, for a vehicle in either of two sizes might operate on the same track-width. To indicate the difference, the 4 mm. system was named OO (Double O) while the HO remained as before. Although the purpose of the OO was to distinguish the scale only we always list OO among the gauges. In practice a gauge description is simply a code which tells us the type of layout. As users of the code, we know that OO is 4 mm. scale and that HO is 3.5 mm. scale throughout.

We also know from the code the actual gauge measurement in millimetres or inches. The OO and HO measurement is 16.5 mm. or about $\frac{5}{8}$ in. If we care to do the arithmetic ourselves we shall find that this is the figure we get from the standard 4 ft. 8$\frac{1}{2}$ in. track-width when each foot becomes 3.5 mm.

"Quite so," some of us may say. "But what about the 4 mm. scale? The 16.5 was intended for 3.5 mm. HO, and if we change the 3.5 to 4 mm. surely we must change the track-width as well? Our slightly larger vehicles are going to look a little odd on the old size of track".

This is precisely what a good many modellers said from the time that OO branched off from HO. Declaring that a new scale demanded a new gauge, they pointed to the backs and fronts of the vehicles on a standard OO layout. "You will observe," they said, "that the vehicles have a somewhat overbodied appearance. Obviously the track should be wider." The Standards Bureau agreed; and still another gauge, the Eighteen Millimetre or EM, was added to the list, as the dissatisfied had long desired.

Thus, to sum up a rather complicated story, the Half-O was enlarged a trifle to provide more room for the motor, and the gauge was then adjusted to agree with the new scale.

From the days of crude tinplate, serious modellers have pressed for greater refinements in the interests of naturalism. Not long after the First World War, Bond's O' Euston Road, R. F. Stedman of Leeds (later the Leeds Model Company) and Mills Brothers of Sheffield earned the respect of O gauge enthusiasts by manufacturing equipment which was more finely to scale than the popular proprietary lines. Very keen modellers, when they could not buy what they wanted, built their layouts to their own requirements, often with the guidance of the progressive model railway magazines. There will always be experimental modellers like these, striving for the best however far off it may be.

Ironically, the use of the metric system for the sake of accuracy has been the cause of certain discrepancies in modelling. A metre is a ten-millionth part of the distance on the earth's surface between Pole and Equator and is not directly linked with the yard, which was originally based on the length of a man's arm. When all our measurements are metric, as in science, they are related only to each other; but the railway measurements of the English-speaking world are in feet and inches and the conversion to millimetres involves a number of decimal places. A metre is 39.37 inches; an inch is 25.400 millimetres. To change metres to inches we multiply by 39.37; to change metres to feet we multiply by 3.281; and to change millimetres to inches we either divide by 25.4 or multiply by 0.03937.

Such calculations may give us a result which is not mathematically exact but is very much finer than we need. Even if we kept to English lengths we should find the decimals stretching away, sometimes endlessly. The correct track-width for $\frac{1}{4}$ in. scale is 1.17708333 in.

There is no difficulty in these conversions beyond the plain arithmetic, and there should seldom be any trouble over the choice of our final figure when we are working to one decimal place from a calculation involving five or six places. What causes the discrepancies is too great a loyalty to the English system. Having found the nearest correct metric measurement, the modelling mathematicians turn affectionately to the nearest equivalent of this in terms of an inch!

At 7 mm. scale a gauge of $56\frac{1}{2}$ in. reduces to 32.958 mm. which can be accepted as 33. But instead of making it 33 the experts decided that it should be 32, because 32 is close to 31.750, the metric equivalent of an inch and a quarter! They went back to their dear old inches, with the consequence that the track-gauge for 7 mm. O is a shade too narrow.

The Standards Bureau expresses most of the dimensions in millimetres. While the conversion from feet and inches must still be made, there is now less temptation to reconvert millimetres into inches or fractions of an inch. If we ever change to inches, as many modellers recommend, the change should be complete and final.

Anyone who checks the EM gauge will discover that 19 mm. (4 mm. to 1 ft. is 1 mm. to 3 in.) is nearer correct than 18. It looks as though the same thing has happened again: as though a step had been taken towards exactness and then back from it in favour of a neat English fraction. But this time the preferred figure rests on a sounder basis. The gauge was fixed at eighteen millimetres to allow for the swing of long outside-cylinder engines on curves. In America, where the wider loading-gauge permits the curves to be sharper, the gauge is nineteen millimetres. As American gauges were correct from the outset, the modellers had no need to deviate into new ones, and consequently their 19 mm. gauge is OO.

Britain's OO was much too firmly established as 16.5 mm. gauge for the Standards Bureau to say that in future OO would mean a gauge of nineteen metres, the track-width proper to 4 mm. scale. At first the Bureau called its new gauge Scale OO in tribute to its correctness.

Here we see a narrower or special use of the word "scale". The beginner who believes that he is working with scale models may be confused when he discovers that this description applies to models of another kind. Before he goes away to brood in a dark corner, let me quickly explain that scale in this sense relates to the fineness of certain measurements. A coarse-scale model is not crudely out of proportion or bare of detail. The coarseness refers to scaling of the wheels, and the measurements as such are extremely small. Coarse-scale models can be very fine indeed!

Many beginners are puzzled on finding that the O scale and gauge are exactly the same as those of OF, the Fine Scale O. Each has a scale of 7 mm. and a track-gauge of 32. Similarly, IF differs not at all in these dimensions—10 mm. scale and 45 mm. track-gauge—from the standard Gauge 1. "But," says the newcomer, "there must be *some* difference." This point is, I hope, now clarified. The special wheel and track dimensions of the fine scales are the only ones affected, and these are not normally listed in a table.

In considering standards, the Bureau took into account the thickness, flange depth and back-to-back spacing of the wheels and also the depth and thickness of the rails. We can have fine-scale track as well as fine-scale rolling stock.

The recommendations of the Bureau have been accepted by the manufacturer members of the Model Engineering Trade Association, the leading makers of scale equipment in Britain. Anything built to B.R.M.S.B. standards (they should be credited to the Bureau and not to M.E.T.A.) is described as being in the scale range and may be used with anything else which conforms to the same scale standards of the Bureau.

Enthusiasts for the finer dimensions are in a minority. As the adherents of railway modelling are extremely numerous, a minority of them may be large; and this is true of the scale-men. They number a great many and the total is increasing. Stimulated by the Bureau and by new manufacturing processes, the trade which specializes in scale products has taken firm shape and grown.

For all that, fine-scale may never become the pursuit of a majority in modelling. It does not appeal to every advanced modeller any more than it appeals to the average beginner.

The preference is purely a matter of taste. It will not in itself create a first-class layout any more than the use of coarser standards will make a first-class layout impossible. The attractiveness of a model railway depends in the end upon the modeller.

Thanks to the enterprise of various companies, the owner of a proprietary system may now adopt finer standards. If he wants his new

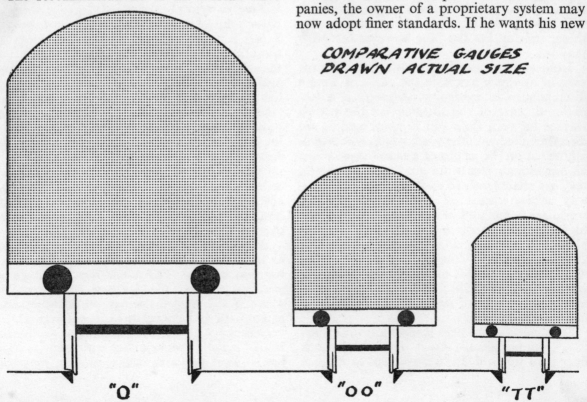

COMPARATIVE GAUGES
DRAWN ACTUAL SIZE

"O"   "OO"   "TT"

track to be of exact scale he can buy wheels of B.R.M.S.B. dimensions and fit them, or have them fitted, in place of the proprietary wheels, which are made to the standards of the particular maker. Scale track by A.B.C., Gem, Hamblings, Killicks, Peco and Romfords is so designed in the interests of accuracy that only vehicles of B.R.M.S.B. specifications (with a back-to-back measurement of 14.50 mm.) can pass through the turnouts and crossings. Rolling stock which would be derailed on this road will travel without difficulty on Universal track because the frogs are differently constructed, the check-rail is a dummy, and the heavy-section rail takes the deepest type of flange. Obviously, then, Universal track is not a correct reproduction. One form is entirely standard; another is standard except for the frogs and switches which are movable; and a third makes an interesting compromise by combining the movable frogs and switches with rail of scale measurements.

Each type offers the owner of a standard railway the chance of laying track which is more realistic. He does not have to discard his existing layout, for the new track will link with the old. It is not always necessary to get the short pieces of adaptor rail manufactured for this purpose. One or two minor adjustments and a little packing with cardboard will set the tracks in line.

Coarse and fine are not so easily mixed in O gauge as in OO. An O gauge locomotive with old-fashioned wheels will come to grief at a true-scale turnout—if, with the deep flanges, it succeeds in running at all. When the wheels are of modern design they should be suitable for flat-bottom track in fine-scale so long as the flangeways at crossings are adjusted. C.C.W. Productions have a fine-scale rail in flat-bottom and bull-head designs. The bull-head is the old type with the rail keyed into chairs on wooden sleepers; the flat-bottom, which will eventually replace the bull-head everywhere in Britain, rests on a baseplate with spring spikes holding the complete unit to the sleeper underneath.

As I have emphasized in another chapter, no one should change to a different kind of track without first weighing all the factors involved. The handiest guide to this complicated subject is G. H. Lake's *Miniature Railways Handbook* (Percival Marshall). G. H. Lake has packed his pages with the highly detailed information which he received as secretary of M.E.T.A.

The technical specifications are not the only points to be studied when a change is contemplated. A proprietary-type modeller attracted by the appearance of scale equipment should bear in mind that the mixture he is considering will differ in looks from the layout in complete scale which he may see at a club or exhibition. Is there anything to be gained from running a scale train on an over-scale track? Can it be said that scale wheels are an improvement to over-scale vehicles?

For the operator of a proprietary layout, the most satisfying use of scale is in the construction of rolling stock from kits. Just as scale wheels may be fitted to standard vehicles, so may the scale bodies be equipped with wheels of standard size. Having built a wagon to scale or near-scale, the modeller buys the proprietary wheels suited to his particular track. As the wagon must in any event have wheels, the cost and work are merely the normal requirements of construction.

We must be grateful to the suppliers of kits and realistic track. They have enriched the modelling movement. But we must not be led into thinking that the makers of the proprietary railways are aloof characters with a take-it-or-leave-it attitude towards the modeller. Some of the critics of the veteran companies talk as though it cost no more to develop a model than to manufacture each of the models patterned upon it. This is fantastically far from the truth. An item for which the buyer pays a few shillings may have cost thousands of pounds before it ever reached the market. An American model railway company spent nearly as much on introducing a new model engine as the full-scale railway had spent on the original.

The aim of the manufacturers is to combine quantity with quality at a marketable price and to make the model so robust, despite the delicacy of the mechanism, that it will last for years. In giving them credit for their success we may remember that railway modelling throughout the world owes its popularity and progress to the proprietary railway, to the boxed set and the accumulated accessories.

You may have heard of a completely new gauge known as S which is larger than OO and smaller than O. All who work in unusual gauges are enormously keen and most of them, including the S addicts, have their own associations.

They deserve our encouragement: it is always pleasant to meet someone who is not doing precisely the same as the neighbours!

No one can tell what gauge or scale will be popular in the future. The last arrival often bounds ahead. Gauge O gained a lead on its bigger brothers and then the timid little OO left all others behind. Already we can see a new challenger, tinier still, moving forward quietly and confidently. Its name is TT, which means table-top and might equally stand for tiny tot.

TT gauge came to Britain from a country where everything is huge. Before the last war Harold Joyce, a model railwayman in Indiana, had to move about a good deal. He badly wanted a layout that would fit into a travelling case so that he could take it with him, and as there was no gauge so small he designed one of his own.

By 1941, when the B.R.M.S.B. first met in England, the railway built for one man's suitcase was being developed for model railwaymen throughout the world. It came before the modelling public at the war's end just as OO was beginning to lead the field. European modellers discovered it in the form of Rokal sets at a scale a little bigger than the American 2.5 mm., and early in 1957 Tri-ang began to pioneer it in Britain as TT3.

What had happened with OO happened again with TT: for practical reasons the manufacturers used a scale which did not agree precisely with the gauge. If we want a 12 mm. gauge the scale should be 2.5 mm. Tri-ang prefers an extra half a millimetre (hence the TT3) with the advantages of better clearances than would be possible in the accurate American scale. The perfectionist dislikes the over-large wheel flanges but admires the perfect smoothness of the running.

There are smaller gauges than TT. Not very long ago OO was called the "jeweller's gauge", and now we have in OOO a railway of half the OO size except for the 9 mm. track-gauge. So far OOO is for a brave minority, but a minority that continues to grow. Smallness has a peculiar fascination. For some people a model can never be too tiny so long as it works. A London watchmaker once built a clockwork locomotive at a gauge of $\frac{1}{8}$ in., and Arthur Sherwood, an old member of the North London Society of Model and Experimental Engineers, likes a steam-driven engine that will go almost into a matchbox, though Australia, where he now lives, has plenty of room for larger models.

Of great promise as a commercial venture is the well-named Liliput, built to European HO standards with a back-to-back measurement of 14.2 mm., flange depth of 1.25 mm., and a plastic base whose curves are of 15 in. and 18 in. radius. The locomotives run on 12-volt direct current, and there is a choice, as in Hornby-Dublo, of two-rail and three-rail track. Tri-ang track may be used and the automatic couplings will fit at least three European makes of rolling stock.

Years ago the first North American enthusiasts for the hobby preferred the OO gauge to the O which was then most popular in Britain. They liked OO so much that it became known as the American or North American gauge. But when the English companies, which were the principal source of the model railway equipment in America—how often we come back to a British source!—brought in OO scale with HO track, the Americans tended towards O gauge partly because the combination did not much appeal to them and partly because they had discovered the positive attractions of the $1\frac{1}{4}$ in. scale. To borrow a title from James Thurber, it became the Wonderful O. Jim Mourning and Bob Rolofson, the authors of *Railroad Modelling* (Trend Books) give the credit for popularizing it to *Model Railway News* "which was widely distributed in the United States".

The fashion next changed in 1936 when Eric La Nal, Dr Alfonse Bacon and George Stock introduced American modellers to the possibilities of HO as a complete scale. HO remains the favourite in America. It is the gauge used by about three-quarters of all model railroaders. TT has jumped to second place. O is now third, and the fourth is S. The modellers remember the gauges in terms of 3-4-6-8: three feet in TT will be four in HO, six in S and eight in O.

It is useful to compare the ratios when we are still planning a layout and have not yet decided upon the size. Thus OO gauge requires about half the space of O and TT just two-thirds the space of OO. To find the minimum size of baseboard we must consider the diameter of a circle constructed in the particular kind of track, for a circle is the smallest continuous layout that we can have. Taking the average radii, the O gauge circle is seven feet in diameter (we must not forget to double the radius) the OO four feet and the TT two. Still smaller circles are common, four feet diameter in O and three in OO, but the average is a reliable guide. For a workable O layout we need, at the minimum, a space of not much less than ten feet by eight, whereas a baseboard of six feet by four will accommodate a OO layout and one only 26 or 27 inches wide will suffice for TT. We shall of course make the baseboard larger than the minimum.

Before we lay track of small radius, we must think ahead to the time when we may want double-track on the curve. If we have 15 in. Hornby-Dublo curves near the edge of the baseboard we shall not have room for 17 in. curves on the outside. The distance in inches between the two inner rails of a double-road, the so-called six-foot way, is taken as $2\frac{1}{4}$ for O gauge curves, $1\frac{3}{8}$ for OO and $1\frac{1}{4}$ for TT. Straight tracks are a little closer: $2\frac{1}{8}$ for O, $1\frac{1}{4}$ for OO, and $1\frac{1}{16}$ for TT.

Of more importance than any correct dimension is the actual degree to which a vehicle overhangs the track. It surprises most beginners to learn that a vehicle is about twice as wide as the gauge. The clearances for ready-made equipment are easily determined, but if we are building to scale on our own, or are buying a scale item such as an Edward Exley coach, we must realize that the clearance and curve-radius may have to be bigger than they would be for proprietary rolling stock.

Ideally, everything on the railway should agree with the operating scale. If four millimetres represent a foot on the engine they should represent a foot elsewhere. As we have seen, the strict fulfilment of this requirement is not always practicable on an ordinary layout. In observing it wherever we reasonably can, we may be helped by having a scale ruler. To make one, we lay a school ruler on a length of cardboard and mark the card at intervals of one foot according to the scale. With OO gauge every four millimetres is indicated as a foot on the cardboard and every two millimetres as six inches. What will ten feet be in OO? We glance at the scale and there is our measurement.

An interesting result is obtained by expressing the scale as a proportion of the foot. To do this we divide. A foot is the equivalent of 304.800 mm. Dividing by four we get 76.200, and so we say that a model in OO gauge is a seventy-sixth of the prototype size. Again and again these figures are given incorrectly through too great a trust in someone's arithmetic years ago.

Now, when we say that a model in 4 mm. scale is a seventy-sixth of the original we obviously do not mean that seventy-six OO locomotives would directly equal a thundering Pacific. We have to think of each part separately in every detail as it would be if magnified by a magician's wand. Our scale measurements are lengths, and therefore a simple division does not introduce the cube for volume. The deeper we go into the mathematics of scale the more complicated and fascinating it all becomes. We can have scale weight, scale power and scale speed.

Speed will interest us if we are running to a timetable. Precisely how it should be calculated provides one of those never-ending arguments on which railway modelling thrives, but we have had enough mathematics for the time and I think many of us will be satisfied if we take 60 m.p.h. as two feet a second for O gauge trains, fourteen inches for OO and ten and a half inches for TT. Most model trains are tremendous record breakers. They sweep along at the equivalent of eighty or ninety miles an hour. But the true scale speeds, disappointingly slow though they seem, improve the realism of the running and are much more convenient for scheduled journeys.

Some modellers adapt an old clock so that it shows the required time interval. A mechanical arrangement is not essential, for we can fix our own intervals and read them from a watch. Using the scale ratio, a minute on an OO railway would correspond to seventy-six minutes on a real line. For a less awkward reckoning we may take a minute as representing an hour. The 9.15 express glides out and one minute later the 10.15 local.

Anyone who becomes muddled and lost in an ordinary published timetable should try reading one of the working timetables issued to railway staff. Every detail is given. The schedules for Western Region alone fill nearly three thousand pages; but there are seventeen sections and so we shall not meet a W.R. guard staggering about with a timetable as big as several volumes of the *Encyclopedia Britannica*!

CHAPTER SIXTEEN

Questions of Power

BETWEEN Paris and Le Mans, among the hills, is a length of permanent way where a train may travel without a driver or any form of direct human control. For an experiment in 1955 French Railways used four empty carriages drawn by their BB9003 electric locomotive, sister of the BB9004 which three weeks earlier had run at 205.6 miles an hour, a new world-record. Transmissions from a radio-control post at Sceaux-Boessé were picked up by a little aerial on the engine. Operating a relay small enough to fit into a waistcoat pocket, they released the brakes, regulated the current to the traction motors, and applied the brakes at the end of the journey. The driverless train reached a speed of 74.5 miles an hour.

Somewhat similar experiments have been carried out in America with a train controlled by low-frequency signals from the telephone wires along the trackside. There and in France the only difficulty is the reluctance of the public to ride in a train without a driver. As an official of French Railways said to me, "*We* are ready but *you* are not".

Thousands of people believe that they would like to go to the Moon, but hardly anyone will step on board a train which is controlled from a few miles away. Meanwhile we have the all-electric model railway to illustrate in miniature the shape of things to come.

A well-developed layout with an electric-type engine may be seen as a picture of to-morrow's railways. Everything mechanical is remotely or automatically controlled. Indeed, modelling has gone further. The Lionel Lines in America feature a remote-controlled milkman; and while this robot figure attends to the delivery of cans from a milk car, horses move down a ramp, herd round a water trough in a trackside corral, and obediently return on a second ramp to their own Santa Fe car.

The whole scene is one of activity. A lumber car rolls its logs into a bin; a travelling crane lowers a magnetic lift, picks up a culvert pipe, and carries the pipe to the goods station; a load of coal dumped from a wagon is hoisted into a bin and tipped into a storage hopper.

Finally the train leaves. The horn sounds on the robust New Haven diesel, smoke curls from the stove in the caboose, red lights flash on the atomic-waste disposal car (Lionel is startlingly up-to-date), signals change automatically, and new train information is flashed from the dispatching board as the attendant in charge crosses the verandah-like structure in front of it.

I hear a sigh from the beginners in Britain. But advanced modellers will say that there is a point at which remote-control and other special effects tend to suggest an electric or mechanical toy rather than a model. This might be their attitude towards the Lionel timber mill. Logs enter the buzzing mill on a remote-controlled conveyor, dressed boards come out on the other

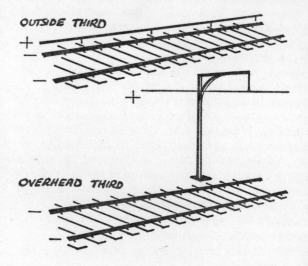

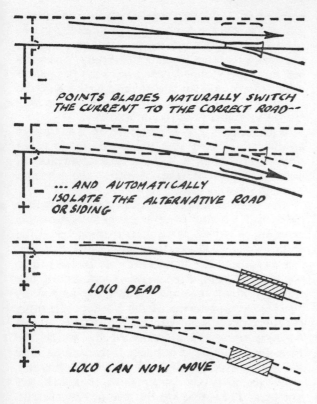

POINTS BLADES NATURALLY SWITCH
THE CURRENT TO THE CORRECT ROAD--

...AND AUTOMATICALLY
ISOLATE THE ALTERNATIVE ROAD
OR SIDING

LOCO DEAD

LOCO CAN NOW MOVE

at one extreme the modeller whose layout is primarily an area for electrical experiment and operation, and if we join a club we may soon find ourselves entangled in wire; but at the other end are the thousands who regard the electricity supply to their layouts much as they regard the water supply in their homes; they take it for granted until it goes wrong.

Let us begin, then, at the beginning. Electricity is a discharge of electrons, the minute particles of energy that dance about the atom. As they belong to all the known matter in the universe, they are not actually made in the electrical apparatus but are brought together and released. This happens in a dynamo where the flow is set up, or induced, by the movement of a wire coil close to the poles of a magnet. It was Faraday who explored the connection between electricity and magnetism and revealed a way of converting mechanical energy, the turning of the coil, into the energy of electric current.

Electricity is also produced by chemical means. To Alessandro Volta, an Italian professor, we owe the discovery that if a piece of copper and a piece of zinc, each with a wire soldered to it, are placed in a glass of weak acid the zinc gradually dissolves, bubbles form on the copper, and a current passes from the zinc to the copper through the liquid, and from the copper to the zinc when the two plates, or electrodes, are joined by a wire. All electric cells work on this principle though they may differ in form.

Most miniature electric railways take their power from either a dry battery or the mains supply. Ordinary household current is produced by dynamos at a generating station. It must in no circumstances be run straight to the layout or to any accessory. The beginner who connects his railway direct to a wall-plug or an electric light flex can expect unhappy consequences. They may indeed be so very unhappy that he knows nothing about them; for mains electricity can kill.

side, and everyone who watches the operation is charmed. Yet many veterans would hesitate, rightly or wrongly, to use such a device themselves. They would place it slightly outside the field of strict modelling; together with the railroad cop in pursuit of a hobo, the newsboy who hands out a paper while a puppy chases its tail round a hydrant, and the gateman who comes out swinging his lantern as the train approaches a level crossing.

Nevertheless it is more than possible that items of similar ingenuity will appear in time on the British-built layout. They are part of a natural development. The Lionel Corporation has a range of clever devices which even the sternest modeller would regard with approval. Having satisfied all the usual demands, it can therefore venture into absolute novelty.

The uses of electricity on a layout are enormously interesting in the applications to remote or automatic control. If we have none of these devices as yet we shall probably work towards them; and in the meantime, assuming that our railway is electric, we should have at least an elementary understanding of electricity as the power which drives the train. Yet this subject is often the last to be properly studied. We meet

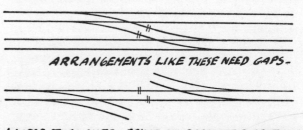

ARRANGEMENTS LIKE THESE NEED GAPS-

WHERE TURNOUTS POINT IN OPPOSITE DIRECTIONS

Before the current reaches the layout it must pass through a transformer. To understand this device we must know the difference between two kinds of current, direct and alternating. While direct current flows like water through a pipe, alternating current surges to and fro.

Now, a transformer consists of two coils, the primary coil and the secondary. Both of them surround the same iron core, but they are not connected electrically. As the current pulsates through the primary coil it sets up a magnetic field whose poles are constantly changing, and this has the effect of creating a current, by induction, in the secondary coil. We are reminded of Faraday and the dynamo, and it may not surprise us to know that, in studying the relationship between magnetism and electricity, Faraday built a kind of transformer. He wound two coils on a block of wood, keeping them apart with layers of twine. Whenever he passed a steady current through the first winding nothing happened, but when he interrupted the flow a galvanometer attached to the second coil showed the presence there of another current which had been induced. His experiment led to the construction of very large coils with as much as two hundred and eighty miles of wire in the secondary winding and with a very rapid make-and-break mechanism to interrupt the primary current.

Unlike this induction coil, the transformer in common use has no need of an interrupter. The current already fluctuates. A steady flow, as Faraday discovered, will pass through the primary coil without affecting the secondary. Consequently our transformer must not be fed with direct current. At best the results will be negative; at worst they will be disastrous.

As a general guide, direct current is the kind that we get from a battery, and alternating current the kind that comes to us from a generating station. But some houses are supplied with D.C. Before we install a transformer we must therefore be absolutely certain that we have A.C. mains. We had better be sure of the voltage as well, in case our local supply differs from the standard—240 in Britain and 110 in the U.S.A.

It is the voltage which is transformed when the alternating current changes to magnetic energy in the first coil and then back to electrical energy in the second. If each coil had the same number of turns, the current issuing from the transformer would be of the same voltage, allowing for incidental losses, as the current entering it. A difference in windings produces a difference in the two voltages, and as this change is the whole purpose of the transformer the wirings are arranged accordingly. The voltage has been stepped down between the generating station and the house; and now inside the house, we step it down further still on the way from the mains plug to our railway.

We amateurs tend to speak of volts as though an electric current were measured in no other way. There are in fact three measurements, all equally important: the quantity, the pressure and the resistance.

Benjamin Franklin thought of electricity as a fluid, and we may for the moment borrow his description, tiresome though it must be to the professional engineer who has read a hundred times that an electric current may be likened to water in a pipe. Electricity is not at all like water. But we may, as laymen, be helped by visualizing it in terms of the household supply from the reservoir. The nature of this supply depends upon the quantity of the water, the pressure at which it is being forced along, and the size of the pipe through which it is flowing.

In electricity the gallons, so to speak, are amperes. They indicate the amount of current. The pressure is shown as volts, and the resistance—the ability of the current to flow—as ohms. Together the three measurements commemorate the work of André Marie Ampère, Alessandro Volta and Georg Simon Ohm: a Frenchman, an Italian and a German.

The degree of resistance is determined by the kind of material through which the current passes, its thickness (the area of its cross-section) and its length and temperature. Some materials, such as copper and silver, allow the current an easy passage; others, such as glass and porcelain, obstruct it almost entirely and on that account are useful when we need a barrier, or insulator. If a length of copper has a resistance of 1.7 ohms, a similar piece of iron or steel at the same temperature will have one of ten and more. Ebonite has billions of times the resistance of copper. Other comparative figures are 1.6 for silver, 2.4 for gold (I doubt if we shall use any) 2.8 for aluminium, 5.8 for zinc, 7.0 for brass, 16.0 for solder and 22.0 for lead.

Like water in a small pipe, current in a thin wire does not move easily. If we push it harder by increasing the pressure, or voltage, the electrons will become agitated and the wire will

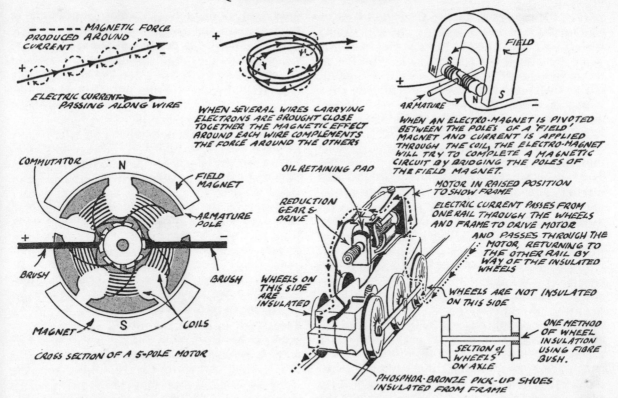

WHEN SEVERAL WIRES CARRYING
ELECTRONS ARE BROUGHT CLOSE
TOGETHER THE MAGNETIC EFFECT
AROUND EACH WIRE COMPLEMENTS
THE FORCE AROUND THE OTHERS

WHEN AN ELECTRO-MAGNET IS PIVOTED
BETWEEN THE POLES OF A 'FIELD'
MAGNET AND CURRENT IS APPLIED
THROUGH THE COIL, THE ELECTRO-MAGNET
WILL TRY TO COMPLETE A MAGNETIC
CIRCUIT BY BRIDGING THE POLES OF
THE FIELD MAGNET.

CROSS SECTION OF A 5-POLE MOTOR

MOTOR IN RAISED POSITION
TO SHOW FRAME

ELECTRIC CURRENT PASSES FROM
ONE RAIL THROUGH THE WHEELS
AND FRAME TO DRIVE MOTOR
AND PASSES THROUGH THE
MOTOR, RETURNING TO
THE OTHER RAIL BY
WAY OF THE INSULATED
WHEELS

WHEELS ARE NOT INSULATED
ON THIS SIDE

ONE METHOD
OF WHEEL
INSULATION
USING FIBRE
BUSH.

SECTION OF
WHEELS
ON AXLE

PHOSPHOR-BRONZE PICK-UP SHOES
INSULATED FROM FRAME

grow warm, like the seat of one's trousers when one slides down a banister. With sufficient resistance the wire glows, thus converting the current into heat. This is the effect we want in the element of a heater or an electric iron. We do not desire it on the layout, and any sign of severe heating must be taken as a signal that something is wrong. A motor may heat but should not be allowed to become so hot that it cannot be held close to the face.

In a large wire the flow is smoother: more power reaches the engine. I also mentioned length as a factor. A long wire has more resistance than a short one and so we shall waste less energy if we keep our wires short. Twists and turns make no difference so far as they affect the length.

Between the amount, the pressure, and the resistance there exists a direct relationship, expressed in Ohm's Law. The pressure equals the amount multiplied by the resistance; or in other words, we can find the voltage by taking the other units, the amps and ohms, and multiplying them.

Most of us are better acquainted with watts than with ohms and amps. The watt is the practical unit for measuring electrical power—

practical in the sense that it forms a convenient measurement for ordinary suppliers and consumers, as distinct from those who do electrical work in a laboratory. It was given its name in 1882, at the suggestion of C. W. Siemens, as a tribute to James Watt who had then been dead for more than sixty years; for Watt showed a great concern for rational measurements and wanted the weights and measures of the world to speak, as he said, the same language.

Wattage is the number of volts multiplied by the number of amps. Like the equation for Ohm's Law, this can be expressed in other ways according to which of the three figures we already know. Taking it straightforwardly, we obtain a figure of twenty-four watts for an engine which consumes two amps at twelve volts. If we know the power requirement in amps of each separate item we can quickly find the total requirement of the layout.

I must assure the beginner who is scared of so much mathematics and so much science that he can keep pretty clear of both, at any rate for the present. It will help him, now or later, to be acquainted with Ohm's Law and to have an understanding of resistance. The track, for instance, is really an extension of the wires; it is part of the circuit, or out-and-back loop, essential to the flow of an electric current. Consequently, we are, in effect, lengthening the wires when we extend the track. The length of wire, as we have noted, affects the resistance; and the tracks, whatever their length, are already composed of a material which does not conduct electricity so easily as copper. We have learnt from Ohm that current, voltage and resistance are directly linked. Given a constant current, an increase in resistance creates a drop in voltage. Here we have the solution to a problem that puzzles and worries many beginners—the apparently mysterious falling off of power on the more distant stretches of the track. Nothing bad is happening. As the resistance rises, the voltage falls and the train runs less smartly than when it is nearer the source of supply. We can cure the trouble by leading supplementary or feeder wires to the weak area. These wires form a by-pass: the current goes straight along them to the other side of the layout without having to encounter the higher resistance of the track metal.

Long before we extend our railway we become interested in controlling the speed of the train. We feel this need early in our railway modelling career. Not only is the speed too high; it is always the same speed. Our train goes as though Casey Jones were in the cab—but even Casey used to slow down before he stopped.

The control is provided by a rheostat. Once again we come back to Ohm's Law, for a rheostat is simply a device for raising or lowering the resistance and so bringing about a corresponding change in the pressure. Coiled inside a box is a length of wire made of an alloy with a high resistance. Turning a handle on the outside moves a contact along the wire. As the contact is live, the current flows into the wire now at one point and now at another. This means that more or less of the high resistance wire is brought into the circuit according to the movement of the knob. When a good length of wire is included we have the effect of a large circuit with a voltage drop that slows the train.

Transformers are controlled by a similar arrangement, a sliding contact which graduates the output by tapping off the turns of wire at a number of points. Having bought the transformer and speed control separately, many modellers like to place them together in a box. While any box will suffice so long as it looks

neat, a business-like appearance is best created by a design which resembles, not too unpleasantly, a school desk. On advanced layouts, particularly at clubs, the lid provides a control panel. This may in time become marvellously complicated. Some of the big American clubs have control panels which seem to have been suggested by science fiction.

At first the box may be open and later it may be fitted with an ordinary lid. The access should be easy from the rear so that the new wires can be led in without trouble. A removable piece of wood makes a convenient back. For still greater convenience the box is sometimes constructed with only three sides or with just two end-walls fixed to a base.

Space should be left for additions and improvements. A power unit with a transformer, as bought at the dealer's, normally includes a rectifier to convert A.C. current into D.C. If our arrangement differs from this a rectifier must be added, unless the locomotive is an exception—such as the Märklin—to the general rule. Fed with alternating current, a permanent-magnet D.C. motor will cook. On the other hand, the usual type of layout may have an auxiliary circuit which supplies alternating current to the solenoids of points and signals.

The solenoid provides another example of electricity converted into magnetism. We can make a simple device of this kind by winding about thirty-five yards of No. 38 s.w.g. enamelled copper wire on a cardboard or paper tube an inch long and three-quarters of an inch in diameter. As the turns must be even, we shall

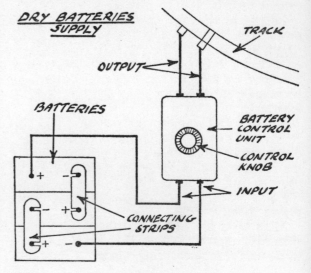

DRY BATTERIES SUPPLY

TRACK

OUTPUT

BATTERIES

BATTERY CONTROL UNIT

CONTROL KNOB

INPUT

CONNECTING STRIPS

find this a hard task. It is better to buy a unit ready-made. We then cut an inch from a six-inch iron nail and place it in the tube, or bobbin, to form the core. It will be heavy enough to move the signal arm at the instant that the current is broken and the magnetism ceases.

Our solenoid signal motor will operate from a battery. Some advanced modellers prefer the D.C. magnet to the A.C. on the ground that it operates more smoothly and at a lower voltage.

Hornby-Dublo has a rectifier-controller unit which gives a twelve-volt direct current for the trains and an alternating current of twelve to sixteen volts for various accessories—but not

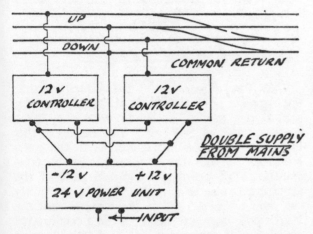

for the travelling post office, an item which must have its own separate supply as is explained in the useful booklet *Hornby-Dublo Three Rail Layouts*. The several control units in this range are of special interest to the operator who wants to run a second train independently of the first. A Hornby-Dublo C-3 controller may be used with an A.C. transformer giving an output of twelve to fifteen volts at one ampere, or with a twelve-volt accumulator.

Any accumulator supplying a model railway should have a capacity, or lasting-time, of at least ten ampere-hours. Like the owner of a radio set in an area without mains electricity, the model railwayman will have two accumulators if he wants to avoid the nuisance of being without power during the period of charging. An accumulator should not be left idle for long when it contains little or no power.

A battery unit has the great merit of neatness and ease of handling. It is excellent for the youngest enthusiasts, but an expanding railway

with its more complicated electrical working calls for a "power pack".

It is simpler in the end to have a transformer unit with several outputs than to take extra leads from a battery unit of conventional design. Confronted with a metal box and two metal-tipped leads rather like bootlaces, the beginner must use his ingenuity if he wants to arrange an alternative circuit. A piece of thick wood fitted with terminals will provide a base for a home-made switch to change the current from one route to another. It is also possible to buy a junction box. But the transformer-rectifier-rheostat unit eliminates the kind of problem that teases the adventurous beginner.

Above all, the household supply is always at our service, ready to be switched on at any moment and never diminishing in strength. I recommend it with one reservation: unless the circumstances are known to be safe, the layout should not be connected to the mains when the current is D.C.

Apart from this exception, the normal electrification of a model railway presents no danger to the person who constructs and operates it with intelligence and care. The lead from the mains must be respected like every other lead from the mains, and it is highly inadvisable for anyone not possessed of the proper electrical knowledge to interfere with any detail of a control unit whether or not it is connected at the time. Sealed boxes should be kept sealed. By enclosing the units and by fitting fuses, cut-outs and red lights the manufacturers have done their best to ensure the safety of the operator and the equipment. In turn, the operator should abide by their clear instructions.

Second-hand and so-called surplus equipment is, on the whole, better left alone unless it is known beyond doubt to be electrically or mechanically reliable. Where doubt exists professional advice should be taken. Every Electricity Board office in Britain will give it readily.

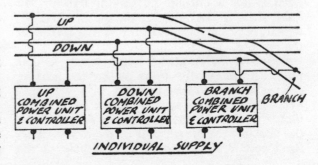

The most important thing on an electric railway is also the most delicate. We have only to look at the interior mechanism of the engine, at the tiny watchlike parts and the thin wires and precisely-adjusted contacts, to realize that here is something that must not be tampered with or in any way treated improperly. Rule No. 1 for all model railwaymen reads: *Take no risks with the motor!*

Let us consider how this mechanism works. An electric motor may be likened to a dynamo which operates the other way round. After Faraday had discovered that an electrical current could be obtained from a magnet by moving a piece of conducting material across the lines of magnetic force, an inventor named Henry Wilde, who is now almost forgotten, built a practical apparatus to obtain electricity in this way instead of from chemical action. In the first experiments coils of wire, wound on a core or drum of soft iron, were revolved between the poles of a magnet. When a conductor moves upward across a magnetic field the current produced flows in a steady direction; when the conductor moves downwards the current flows the opposite way. We can therefore guess what happens in a dynamo. Revolve a wheel on a horizontal shaft and every spoke will go up on one side and down on the other; therefore at the middle point where the armature or rotating coil of a dynamo turns over the current reverses. The very rapid change gives us alternating current unless the pulses are corrected.

Instead of making electricity, an electric motor is supplied with it; and the armature, which in the dynamo is driven round to produce the current, can drive another mechanism. One end of a magnet is its South pole and the other its North (the Earth itself is a huge magnet) and the two have opposite characters. There are really two magnets in our motor; for the armature, like any coil of the kind, becomes magnetized when a current passes through it. We have, then, a fixed magnet and another magnet which rotates and depends for its magnetism on the current.

Opposite poles attract each other; similar poles are unfriendly. If we picture the moving coil as a bar wrapped round with wire and balanced like a see-saw, we easily see how the motor works. At the instant that we switch on the current, the North pole of the now-magnetized coil is drawn to the South pole of the

fixed magnet and is also thrust in that direction by the North; and there is a similar action at the other end. The coil revolves, together with the axle to which it is fixed. Electrical force has been turned into magnetic force and then into mechanical.

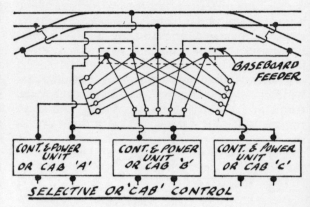

BASEBOARD FEEDER

CONT. & POWER UNIT OR CAB 'A'

CONT. & POWER UNIT OR CAB 'B'

CONT. & POWER UNIT OR CAB 'C'

SELECTIVE OR 'CAB' CONTROL

"Yes," says someone, "I can understand that the opposite poles would be attracted, but why should the motion continue once they have come as close as they can?" The answer to this important question introduces us to the commutator. So that the armature may be constantly pulled around, the South pole of the armature is altered to a North pole at exactly the right moment; and in the same instant the North pole changes. The result is a continuous rotation of the armature and its shaft as long as power flows into the motor.

Through the commutator, the armature reverses its polarity at great speed as it turns. Let us imagine a flat ring of copper cut in half and wrapped about a spindle which is too fat for it. The spindle revolves and a contact presses against the ring—except at the places where the two halves fail to meet. With suitable electrical connections the broken ring thus becomes a kind of revolving switch which reverses the polarity of the armature by changing the direction of the current. The contact is provided by brushes.

A commutator may be used on a dynamo to convert A.C. into D.C. Alternating current cannot be used for the permanent-magnet motor which I have described because the polarity of the flow is changing all the time, not at the motor's rate but at the rate set by the generating station. Series-wound and shunt-wound motors will run on A.C. as they are so designed that the pulse of the current changes the polarity of both armature and magnet at the one time. These types are combined in the compound-wound motor.

The armature of a permanent-magnet motor will in practice have three or more poles instead of the two in our elementary example. As motors are often magnetized after they have been assembled, the removal of the armature, even for a second, will cause a loss of power. Dropping a magnet may also weaken it. Serious failures can be detected by an ammeter, the instrument for measuring amperes: the reading will be higher than is normal for a given load. All advice on this subject can be summed up in two words: *Don't meddle*. Our intimacy with the motor should consist of lubricating and cleaning it according to the instructions. If something is wrong it can very likely be put right by the makers.

An apparent failure of the motor may be caused by trouble on the line. The track is part of the circuit—all of it in fact, except for the wires connecting the rails to the source of power. Unless the circuit is complete a current will not flow, for it is of the nature of electricity that it must return whence it came. Supposing we remove a wire while the train is running; at once the train stops. A gap at any point makes the circuit ineffective. We all know this—we all know it, and yet we often fail to apply it logically when a fault occurs. Motor, controller, power source—everything comes under suspicion until, moved by a last faint hope, we examine the rails. The motor will not have to be sent away; the transformer has not burned out; the battery is not dead; the generating station has not broken down—but two rails have a tiny gap between them!

Two big gaps occur on every model railway, one of them at the control end and the other between the rails which are insulated from each other. The first break is closed when we move the switch to On, and the second when a locomotive stands on the track. By making a bridge between two rails the engine itself becomes part of the circuit as much as the wires and rails.

We will trace the path of the current on a two-rail layout. From the power source, electricity passes to the rail, travels along it, runs up a wheel and into the motor, flows out through a wheel to the rail on the opposite side, and comes home again. Insulation sets the required route through the engine by preventing the current from going anywhere else. Plastic is

sometimes used for this purpose on wheel rims or near the hubs. Without insulation the electricity would run through all the wheels and through the frame: the whole locomotive would be live.

In the three-wheel system the third rail is insulated from the two running rails which are themselves not insulated from each other. A shoe, brush or spoon underneath the engine picks up the current from the third rail, and passes it through the motor, to both rails, by way of the wheel contact. As these rails are electrically connected, in one of them a gap at a turnout or crossing does not affect the flow; the return or negative path remains unbroken so far as the actual circuit is concerned. In two-rail operation the blades and frogs at turnouts have to be isolated to prevent short circuits and at the same time must offer a continuous route for the current.

The third rail may lie between the running rails or be on the outside as in Southern Railway practice. When it is on the inside it may be level with the others or slightly higher. It is usually level in OO gauge. We find the raised rail oftener in O gauge, and in the outside-rail system on the Southern Railway pattern. The higher outside rail rests on insulators and the current is picked up by collectors projecting at each side.

We now know what is meant by all-level centre third, raised centre-third and outside-third. Trix offers us yet another arrangement, double two-rail. On a Trix railway the third rail provides the return. The other rails are insulated from it and from each other, with the result that the layout can use two circuits for two engines. One engine picks up the current from the left-hand running rail and sends it back through the centre rail; the other takes its supply from the right-hand rail and sends it back on the same central route, for two circuits can have a common return. So it is that two Trix trains, the Trix Twin Cadets, can run on one track at the same time. Through separate power units they may be sent in different directions at different speeds.

Another form of electrification, the stud-contact system, was inspired by the Hastings Tramway. The centre-rail is replaced by a row of fine studs wired under the sleepers. After taking the current from these contacts, the locomotive returns it through both the other rails.

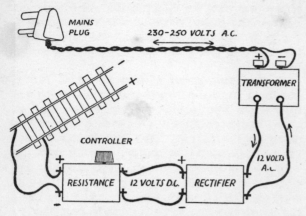

If we are looking for something different but not beyond our scope, we may like the idea of an overhead railway. This is really a three-rail arrangement with the difference that the third rail has become a wire suspended above the track. The engine carries on its roof a spring-loaded collector, the pantograph, which can be raised and lowered. From the wire, or catenary, the current flows through the pantograph to the motor and back through one of the rails.

Overhead-third has long been used for inter-urban trolley-cars in America and therefore is frequently seen on the models of these cars. As British Railways are re-introducing it, and as models may now be obtained from Tri-ang and Trix as well as from Märklin and Bradshaw, more and more towers are going to spring up on British layouts.

Eventually a model railway comes to have two systems of electrification, the one which it was born with and the one which it has acquired in the course of growth. To the basic control of the train we add the control of other things. Points, signals, turntables and travelling post offices do not mark the end of our electrification programme; for some they do not mark even the beginning. The enthusiast who would rather have a second locomotive than a dozen remote-controlled points will be concerned at an early stage with providing a second running-circuit unless he has a Trix layout or something similar.

The secret of the Trix railway is that by employing the centre rail as common return, and by insulating the running rails from each other, it fits two circuits into one layout. For the independent operation of two engines we must have two circuits, and if they are not built into the track we have to devise them ourselves.

However much we overwork our thinking-boxes we shall not escape the fundamental truths of electricity. A current takes the path open to it. Allow two currents to meet, as they will at the first chance, and they are instantly one. Thus the two circuits essential for fully independent working are denied us so long as there is no gap to prevent the meeting. Our original system has then been doubled but not altered. We are running two railways as a single unit and each of them is in no way changed. If we think in terms of two-trains-two railways we have a complete guide to what we require and what we expect. We know that each train needs its separate power and control and behaves as an independent train only when it has its own circuit.

The two work in different sections but they can change places. If the gaps separating the circuits occur at a point where two lengths of track are normally joined, a plastic pin or a matchstick may be inserted to keep the lengths apart electrically and together structurally. When we cut a gap in a rail for a signalling effect, we usually fill the space with modelling cement or a tiny piece of cardboard to make sure that the severed ends will not touch. The gap is always small. An engine approaching it will travel until the last instant that it receives power from that section; in other words, it travels itself out of contact—which means that it makes contact with the next length of rail just enough for the second circuit to energize the motor.

If the engine, having entered the other section, is then deprived of power it will remain isolated. Nothing outside the section can affect it until the power is restored to that part of the track. Once again the wheels roll over the insulation to be carried forward by the current on the other side.

A dead section like this increases the interest and efficiency of a siding or branch line. It is also employed, with the adjoining sections carrying constant power, to provide through-running on the section or block pattern. The current on both sides of the gap must correspond. Are the positive rails in line? We must have the same polarity. Are the transformers in phase? We must have the same voltage; which means, with two transformers, that the positive and negative peaks of their cycles are set to coincide.

"What's this?" you say. "Ohm's Law was

The Pennsylvania Railroad popped 6,000 flash bulbs for this centenary picture of the Horseshoe Curve at night.

This pantograph works. Steeplecab in OO/HO gauge.

Single track level-crossing.

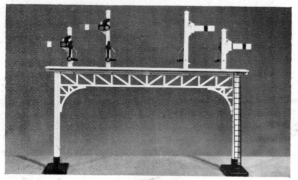

Signal gantry.

Transcontinental electric locomotive with headlights.

Something different—a well wagon in TT.

TT girder bridge for single track.

Right- and left-hand points.

Low-sided TT wagon   (*Tri-ang pictures*)

Here they go! Wagons on the tip-yard hump at Whitemoor marshalling yard.

Here they come! Whitemoor is near Cambridge.

(*British Railways*)

Tony Appleby of Westcliff-on-Sea who built masterpieces when he was a schoolboy.

After driving a passenger train for 50 years William Jones has own Wildcat Railway in California. Walt Disney likes to come over for a ride.

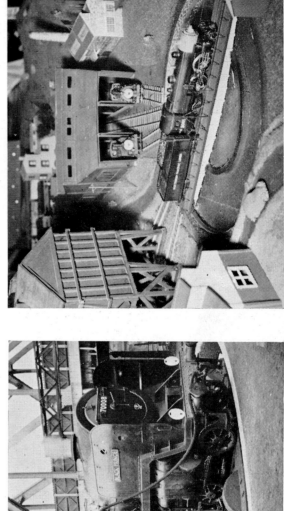

George Boffin of Leicester began with O gauge clockwork. This is the turntable

B.R. Class 7 4-6-2 locomotive No. 70008 "Black Prince" on the turntable at

Model railway at the great Franklin Institute in Philadelphia.

(Jules Schick)

Top: Shanti Goonewardene, aged 14, running his Hornby "Silver King" and goods with his brothers Saliya (9) and Sriyantha (4) at their home in Colombo. *Below*: The same idea in Britain. Vernon Jeffery of Cuffley, Herts, with his layout (*left*) and Michel Broussine of Forres. Is there any country in the world without model trains?

Real railway or model? We may hesitate over our answer when . . .

W. S. Norris shows us pictures of his Stroudley line in O gauge.

enough; the phasing of transformers is too much. If I have to be an electrician as well as a mathematician I shall take to basket-weaving or the trombone." The alarm is groundless. Nine out of ten beginners are happy with proprietary equipment or a standard variation from it. Everything has been made as simple and straightforward as it can be, and our knowledge of electricity need not go beyond the point of knowing what we are about. An understanding of the principles involved in even an elementary electric layout will save us from mistakes which may be serious, besides showing us what we may do as we advance. It is not hard to grasp the principles of electricity (or of most other subjects) if we refuse to be frightened off by an unfamiliar word or idea.

I advise the novice to move forward slowly. Electrical constructions which look thrillingly attractive in theory are apt to shed their delightfulness in practice. It is possible, for example, to connect a signal motor to a short piece of insulated rail in such a way that the solenoid is energized by every vehicle in contact with the rail but is operated only by the first vehicle of the train. A counterweight, falling over its own centre of gravity as soon as a locomotive enters the length, cuts off the current to itself and at the same time switches on the current to an opposing magnet which returns the signal arm as the train moves out of the block. This solves an old problem; but unless we are uncommonly good at making small electrical gadgets which will operate precisely, we may think that it solves nothing for ourselves. There is no department of railway modelling more fascinating than the electrical; and none more exasperating.

Proprietary equipment relieves us of complexities. Section insulation is provided at points in both Hornby-Dublo and Tri-ang, and the Hornby-Dublo insulating rails and tabs have a place in many layout designs. Anyone getting the equipment will of course follow the instructions supplied. Each locomotive as we know, requires a separate controller and the two must be set to give the same direction of travel when a train is transferred from one circuit to another. Self-isolating points act as a switch between two circuits. If we keep this idea of two circuits always in our minds we shall have no difficulty.

Hornby Dublo, Tri-ang, Trix Twin, Rivarossi, Liliput and the principal American makes

all operate on a basis of twelve volts D.C. Märklin locomotives will also take this current though they are intended for A.C. at twenty volts. Each Märklin engine has an auxiliary hand-reversing lever which takes the place of remote-control reversing when the D.C. current is connected. Remote-control will then not work unless a special conversion has been made.

The amperage rating is 0.75 to 1.0 for Hornby-Dublo, 0.50 for Tri-ang, 1.0 to 1.5 for Trix Twin, 1.0 to 1.5 for Märklin, 0.25 for Rivarossi, 1.0 to 1.5 for the Bassett-Lowke motor on full load at 12 volt D.C.; and generally about 0.25 for scale models, British, American and Continental. All are approximate.

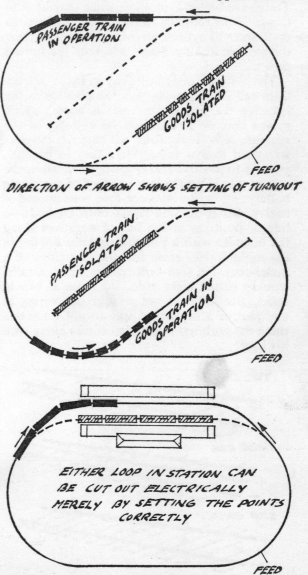

PASSENGER TRAIN IN OPERATION
GOODS TRAIN ISOLATED
FEED
DIRECTION OF ARROW SHOWS SETTING OF TURNOUT

PASSENGER TRAIN ISOLATED
GOODS TRAIN IN OPERATION
FEED

EITHER LOOP IN STATION CAN BE CUT OUT ELECTRICALLY MERELY BY SETTING THE POINTS CORRECTLY
FEED

◄ Borchester Station, on a realistically operated model line in OO gauge.

The American ratings vary from Pennsylvania Scale and Kemtron at 0.3 to Kendrick and Davis at 5.0 for a particular model.

Upon these amperes depends the pulling force. It takes more to start an engine than to keep it going, and once we have it going the excess power develops the speed. This is the rolling load, as distinct from the starting or stalling load before the engine moved.

In electricity we never get something for nothing. A bigger load demands more power. Gradients should be gentle (not more than 1 in 40, or a rise of three inches in a distance of ten feet) and if the engine is not receiving the necessary surplus of power the load must be reduced. Trains are better kept short when they have to climb. If the red button on the controller pops up to warn us against an overload we must clear the trouble at once—and not keep the button down.

The batteries must be linked up as the instructions tell us. When we join the positive to the negative we are connecting in series, which means that we are adding the voltages of the separate cells. Three four-volt batteries in series will yield twelve volts. Were they in parallel, positive to positive and negative to negative, the output would be the same as that of any single battery; or, in this instance, four volts instead of twelve. Series-parallel mixes both methods—a line of positives and a line of negatives along the outsides with a positive-negative linking in the middle, criss-cross like the fastenings of a duffel-coat. Six four-volt cells in series-parallel would provide eight volts, the same as two in series. But however we arrange our wiring in any part of a layout we still do not get something for nothing. Herr Ohm comes along with his Law!

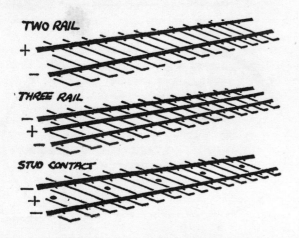

Wiring in parallel is useful for lineside accessories. It has the great advantage that a particular accessory may be switched off without breaking the circuit. We all know the Christmas tree lights which are so arranged, like daisies on a chain, that if one goes out they all go out. This is series wiring. With parallel windings we should still have eleven lights when the twelfth one decided that Christmas was too much for it.

Most of the popular British makes of model railway now use two-rail. Hornby-Dublo has both systems. As an engine designed to pick up current from a third rail will obviously not work without the third, a conversion is necessary before an old locomotive will run on the new track. Rivarossi locomotives may be converted the other way, to three-rail. Liliput provides for both types, and we also have a choice in Märklin—of ordinary centre-rail or stud-contact.

The beginner who has no great wish to experiment with electrical luxuries may yet like to install a feeder scheme, or a scheme for bonding the rails on one side to give the current an easier passage. I prefer feeders as they can be led under the baseboard (the right place for wires) to various points on the track where we wish to refresh the supply. The wire should be of copper and not smaller than No. 18. Tinplate tubular rail has more than five times the resistance of steel solid rail, and so the layout is correspondingly larger in relation to the power. It soon needs feeders.

There are men who would rather dig up the garden and distemper the whole house than solder the handle of a saucepan. Much of the difficulty is imagined; inspired by dislike of handling a hot iron (an object with sinister associations for our ancestors in the Middle Ages) the notion that only a few can do it has been passed along like a rumour. Perhaps only a few can do it well. But nearly everyone can make a join which will survive mild treatment.

The surfaces are cleaned and coated with a suitable flux. In attaching a feeder the iron is held at the intended join until both wire and rail are hot, and the solder is then applied so that it flows between them. After a while, when the solder looks smooth, the iron may be taken off and a stick pressed on the wire to keep it in place. The two most important rules are that the iron must be really hot and that the connection must not be disturbed until the solder is cool. Be careful where you leave the hot iron, try not to drop solder in the wrong places, and clean all traces of chemical from the finished work.

As everyone will read the instructions provided with most items, or obtainable direct from the makers, I shall not outline them here except to emphasize the need for cleanliness and regular moderate oiling. Providing that the instructions are obeyed, any breakdown which occurs is probably not serious. Our first thought should be of connections. Is there a faulty connection somewhere, or one which should not be there at all? Any bad join along the wire or the track—a loose terminal, a rail which has worked away from its fellow—will stop the current. An unwanted connection may have a worse effect, for then we have a short circuit. This occurs when we accidentally lay a screwdriver or other metal object across the rails or when someone, in a bright spirit of experiment, tries to run an old tin engine. Other causes are over-tightness of the baseboard screws, bending of the centre-rail (if there is one) and the sliding of a centre-rail connecting-plate between the insulating plate and the bottom of the rail base. We may also be double-heading with an engine the wrong way round.

The possible sources of trouble can be eliminated in order. If there is apparently no fault in the track-circuit, the engine must be suspected. Will it work when it is off the track? The motor may be over-oiled and have to be slowly dried: the commutator may need cleaning. If nothing seems to be amiss here, we must check the power unit. Has a fuse blown?

Self-insulating turnouts divide the layout into neat areas for inspection. We can also examine the track by wiring a suitable lamp to a couple of clips or other contacts which are then slid along the rails which normally carry current. If the trouble is a falling off in power we may clean the rails with Thawpit and see if the running improves. It is amazing what an effect ordinary cleaning often has on anything used in electricity.

The method of electrification used by the beginner is known as Single Supply. It takes the same form whether the tracks themselves are single or double, except of course that in double-working the Up and Down roads are entirely separate with complete breaks in the continuity of all the rails at the crossover. Double Supply is more complicated. It used to be known as Split Potential because the current of twenty-four volts is divided into negative and positive halves, with a common rail. Individual Supply combines Single and Double. Of more interest to many, though not on the whole to beginners, is Selective Supply for the running of several locomotives independently on one track, though not with more than one of them in the same section at once. As each engine is directed throughout the journey by its own controller, Americans call the method Cab Control. For some incredible reason of purchase tax, the name could not be adopted by the trade in Britain. The B.R.M.S.B. settled for Selective Supply, which will do well enough.

All three systems are outlined in the *Miniature Railways Handbook*. For the person who is progressing from the elementary stage to the advanced nothing could be clearer and brighter than *How to Wire Your Model Railroad* by Linn H. Westcott (Kalmbach). This booklet begins by assuming, more or less, that you have never heard of electricity, and leaves you all set to take over as the club expert.

Nothing smaller than a volume of the *Encyclopaedia Britannica* could contain the whole of this subject, the electrification of a model railway. It relates fundamentally to the running of the trains and is involved in all kinds of refinements from signalling to train lights and engine-whistle; all of which is appropriate to our electrical age. Seated before the master control of a miniature railway system, the operator dispatches a slow freight along the country branch-line, speeds up the mail, swings the turntable for the tank engine in a dead section, and briskly manipulates the points and signals. He has achieved C.T.C., Central Traffic Control, with certain elements that are closer to the future, to that stretch of line which is ready for us—when *we* are ready—among the hills of France.

CHAPTER SEVENTEEN

Completing the Picture

LOOK out of the train window. Not long ago we left the ragged edge of a city with a new box-like factory every few hundred yards along the busy, ugly, self-important main road; and then we passed through a level countryside of sedgy meadows, big trees, quiet old towns and an occasional river too lazy to care much about reaching the sea. Here all is different. There are hills now on either side. Farmhouses sit in tilted fields, and cows loiter by the sloe-bushes on the side of thin, hurrying streams. It might be a new country. But it is still England; and there are more changes yet to come as the train sweeps us onward.

By the time that we arrive we may be full of ideas for our miniature railway. A layout without scenery can never be realistic. Incredibly, the modeller who worries about a quarter of a millimetre on a wheel-flange is often the very one who operates a model railway quite unlike any actual railway on the earth's surface. Pondering a detail which few would notice, he ignores the shrieking total effect of trains in a void. It surprises me still more that some of the larger clubs provide their layouts with no environment except the mechanical one. They will say that they are interested primarily in running, and there can be no doubt that the actual operation of the trains engrosses them. But surely this attitude is lop-sided? If landscape may be ignored on the ground that it is not necessary to correct running, so may a score of other refinements. The chimney of an electrically-driven model steam engine is not necessary to its performance.

A layout should look attractive. However pleasing it may be on the mechanical side, it can obviously be made to look better by the addition of scenery and buildings. The improvement satisfies the operator and the person who comes casually to watch. A modest railway with landscape will interest the average man and woman far more than an elaborate arrangement set in a barrenness of wood. When I was a boy, fairground crowds would gather to watch a model of a Cornish tin-mine at work. The people liked it because it looked so much like the real thing— and is this not the aim and the fascination of all modelling? It is what the public expects and finds at every *Model Engineer* National Models Exhibition and at the smaller provincial shows. The child who dots his toy railway with little figures of animals and buildings made of paper is answering the old human instinct which impelled the cave-men to scratch the world's first pictures on their walls of rock.

Scenery on a layout catches the interest of people who are not normally enthralled by model trains. What the modeller has created is a picture which everyone can enjoy, from the youngest little girl to the oldest old lady who comes to tea. The picture was always there, in the railway itself; and now it is complete.

I know a distinguished historical novelist who begins the last chapter of a book as soon as he finishes the first, and is then happy and confident; for all that he has to do, he says, is to fill the stretch between! A modeller may adapt this idea. There is no reason why the scenery should not be built immediately after the track-laying. On the contrary, the scenery and the track are so intimately connected that it is a mistake to think of them as separate projects. They should be planned together even if they are not laid at the same period. The absence of scenery on some highly developed layouts is explained by the impossibility of fitting it at the present stage. Placed at random on the baseboard, a hill would represent one of the geological wonders of the world.

Many first-class modellers regret that in their eagerness to run the trains they failed to provide for a landscape. "Scenery? I can add that at any time." But in fact scenery is one part of a model railway that cannot be added at will. The steepest hill blends into the ground at its base; the shortest tunnel must have a purpose for existing.

We should therefore visualize the surroundings before we fix the track. Once the railway has begun to grow, the provision of scenery will become more difficult unless we keep our eyes steadily on the finished picture. Sufficient space must be left, especially at the back. Even with planning, we shall probably have to take up some of the track and reorganize one or two areas. But we do not want to uproot a settled layout entirely when all the wiring and fixed accessories are firmly in place. An established railway can be so complex that it would break the owner's heart to tear it up again.

As Edward Beal points out towards the end of *Railway Modelling in Miniature* (Percival Marshall) the ideal scheme "closely approaches the very reverse" of the common practice among layout designers. As Nature was here before the railway, we can present a logical case for beginning with the landscape. At any rate, the person who is planning a railway in his mind as a project for the future has a great opportunity and may end with an adequate layout. The modeller who always intends to add a complement of scenery is like the settler in Arkansas who intended to mend his roof, but either the weather was too bad or the hole gave him no trouble.

In any event the scenery should *appear* to have been there first. I am afraid that it can all too easily look like an afterthought whether it is or not. This is the hardest part of our task—to create the impression that the scenery belongs there and that the railway was built to follow its contours. The shapes are more important than the colours and textures, for our problem is mainly one of proportion.

We must first choose the kind of territory that we want. The choice is unlimited. In making a decision, we can draw a line between the rural and the urban, between a landscape which will be thick with buildings and one which will consist in the main of open country. It is the second of these which suits the beginner.

I return to my idea of an island railway. If the peculiarities of an island are helpful to the beginner in explaining certain oddities of route and operation, they are an equal or greater aid in designing the scenery. The modeller is not, for instance, confronted with the difficulty of suggesting two or more good-sized towns. The special character of the island gives him licence to attempt effects which fit his limitations and yet are not improbable. Here is a train coming out of a tunnel. We are seeing it on its way from the island capital, hidden behind a range of hills. Few people live on this side, but the whole community must be served. What really justifies the railway is the prosperous mine up there on the slopes; an engine-house with a scattering of crude buildings. Because of the mine, the train frequently takes an upper-level track.

In a scheme of this kind the hills will be at the rear. If the baseboard stands close to a wall the possibilities are excellent, for then we can bring the wall into the scenery as a means of giving it depth. Ideally the wall should be painted to represent sky and also, perhaps, a further range of hills on the horizon. In homes where mural painting is discouraged the background may be a board, cloth, or sheet of paper—preferably board as this will not show any creases. The hills are shaped like loaves which have been cut in half. With their flat sides right against the wall or board they create the impression of a whole vista.

For a layout approachable on all four sides, it is generally better to make the hills complete. Hills are not essential. The countryside may be flat or gently undulating. But if we want a tunnel—and who can resist one?—we must have the kind of landscape that justifies it. A tunnel standing in the middle of nothing is still the cereal box of the six-year-old, no matter how much camouflage we apply. We shall, I think, prefer some degree of hilliness. Mountains are vastly attractive, but we must bear in mind that they must slope naturally into the lower ground. There is scope for abrupt hills if we are modelling the china-clay area of Cornwall, with its huge white peaks: a promising subject for an industrial landscape.

Unless we are content with a flat expanse (which can be charming) we shall need to fit another surface on to the baseboard whether our countryside is mild or dramatic. This groundwork, as we may call it with special truth, can be constructed in any one of several ways. The basic pattern is always the same: a supporting structure overlaid with a material which can be arranged in the required shapes.

We begin by setting up the supports. All that we want is a rough framework capable of holding the material that will represent the rise and fall of the ground. It may be built of wood or metal or shaped from wire coat-hangers. Over it we lay a covering broadly fashioned to the contours that we have planned.

The covering must hold a top layer of plaster or *pâpier-maché*. It should therefore be sturdy. Some modellers favour the kind of screen wire which is used for pantry windows in England and for outer doors in countries which are accustomed to an annual summer. Having bought a sheet from the ironmonger, we place it over the frame and cut it with a pair of pliers as needed. It is as well to use gloves.

Other suitable materials are hardware cloth of about a quarter-inch mesh and canvas or burlap. For cheapness there is nothing better than cardboard cut into strips. The pieces are placed over the framework and fastened together by pins, strong adhesive or paper staples. Brown paper is sometimes spread over the whole.

Still better results in contouring can be expected from the use of paper towels. Small strips about two inches by three are dipped into water and then into a thin paste. One layer spread on another, to make about six layers in all, will give the framework a tough covering which can be painted as it is if we prefer not to meddle with plaster. Indeed, the effect may be so attractive that those who had intended to apply plaster or *pâpier-maché* will change their plans.

Old cloth towels are yet another possibility. The best procedure is to experiment with whatever materials are easiest to get. On an ordinary layout the structure will not be large, and so we have no need to think in terms of a complicated and messy project. We are still working in miniature and our problem is to keep on the small side all the time. Scenery built without a constant regard for proportion will startlingly resemble the Mountains of the Moon.

Building or patching plaster will provide a surface which can either be moulded while it is wet or carved when it is dry. Either kind may be mixed with asbestos plaster, preferably half-and-half. The asbestos provides strength and roughness. Warm water often gives a better mixture than cold. To make the stuff set fairly quickly we use half water and half vinegar, stirring them together before we mix. The plaster will then harden in about two hours instead of six. If for some reason we want to slow the process we omit the vinegar and add salt. Pieces of dry plaster will not join successfully.

The normal practice in mixing is to take a bowl about half-full of water, stir it gently, and pour the plaster in slowly and carefully so that no air bubbles are formed. Continuous stirring, always in the same direction, produces a creamy mixture which can then be thickened by adding more plaster or thinned by pouring in more water. It should spread easily without being so thin that it runs and drips. Experiment will show us the right consistency.

Modelling cement may be bought at the dealer's and we may like to get it there instead of looking for two plasters, such as gypsum and alabaster, and then stirring them together. Alabastine, Alabastone, Polyfilla and Pyruma are much used. Anyone who buys a mix will naturally follow the directions intended for it, as they will, I hope, with everything that I have mentioned in this book.

While excellent new preparations appear in the shops, some of us will fall back on a very old material. Dolls of *pâpier-maché*, the Frenchman's "chewed paper", were cherished long ago by little girls in the Far East, and puppets of the same substance are made in our schools today. We tear some newspapers into squares of an inch or less, soak the bits in water for about forty-eight hours, and then stir in a thick paste of starch and water—a cup of starch to a quart of hot water for a bucketful of the *pâpier-maché*. When the starch has thoroughly soaked into the paper the stuff is spread over the framework to a depth of a quarter of an inch or more. It looks like a mysterious kind of porridge and a hungry person who sees it in the saucepan is bound to wonder.

Flour or plaster-of-Paris may be added to the porridge if we desire. Plaster-of-Paris on its own forms an excellent covering. A sixpenny or shilling packet may help us at various points on the layout, particularly when we wish to model a small feature after the main contours are finished.

As *pâpier-maché* takes a week or ten days to harden, we have plenty of time to work on it. We should not apply any paint until it is completely dry. Fences, trees, rocks (corks or real stones) can be planted where they are needed and allowed to take root as the mixture sets. If nails are driven into the base the plaster will stick to them. The framework itself is usually fixed to the baseboard with nails or adhesive.

Before the plaster sets we check for fingerprints. At this stage we may like to sprinkle the landscape with a handful of dry plaster. This, when it is painted, will make the surface look more like earth.

What paint shall we use? The choice is largely an individual one. Some people are happy with oils and others with water colours. Either kind will suit the layout scenery, but if we distemper the wall at the back we shall need oil paint. Students' oil colours are reasonably priced and are obtainable in small tubes. They are mixed with turpentine or turpentine substitute. For poster paints, which many of us will prefer for all the ordinary landscape, the mixing agent is water.

The principal colours that we require for the soil include burnt umber, raw umber, burnt sienna, raw sienna, Van Dyck brown, chrome green (dark), cobalt blue, chrome yellow and possibly vermilion and black. Raw umber, burnt umber and Van Dyck brown will give us normal brown soil; burnt sienna and burnt umber mixed will produce a richer brown. For grey granite we may apply pale ultramarine blue to a thin wash of lamp black. Grey limestone is suggested by a thinner wash of the lamp black and a lighter touch of the blue. If paint can be worked into the plaster before the mixing, no white patches will show through anywhere.

Grass is represented by grasspaper glued to the surface, by fine sandpaper painted green, by medical lint similarly treated, or by coloured sawdust. The sawdust is either dyed and sprinkled on to wet glue, or is left in its natural colour and spread on wet green paint. Green grass flock, if we use it, should not be inhaled.

By varying the colour of the sawdust we can represent various crops as they would be seen from a fair distance. Oats, barley and wheat are shown by bits of sisal string stuck to the base. Between the fields we erect little hedges of wirewool, coloured sponge (is there an old loofah in the house?) or twigs. A hedge in England may be anything from a thin line of bushes to a green rampart of earth and stone.

Trees are either bought at the dealer's or modelled at home. We make them from wire, twigs or weeds. The wire method is the hardest and often the least satisfactory. I recommend twigs, weeds, or Norwegian lichen. The twigs are coated with glue, dipped into sawdust or

tea-leaves, and coloured green. Weeds or moss may be dyed or painted as soon as they are gathered or they may first be pickled. The pickling fluid is made of two parts water to one part glycerine and is heated to just under boiling-point. After being soaked in warm water the weeds are placed in the fluid for at least forty minutes. The effect is sometimes better if they stay there overnight.

Yarrow is a useful weed for O gauge. Much depends of course upon the particular type of tree that we want. For some kinds we may use a sprig of heather, for others, a quantity of Norwegian lichen from the dealer's, and for others again a piece of sponge or some Ozofern from Boots.

The quickest way to represent water is to paint it on the base in suitable blues and greens. Glass may be laid above it, but this is not essential. If painted glass is used the paint should be on the underside. Ripple glass, celluloid, waterglass, cellophane, shellacked plaster, sheet plywood rippled with plastic wood, liquid casting plastic: all these materials are seen on model railways where water is represented, flowing or still. Now and then we may even see a layout with real water!

A river or lake provides a reason for a bridge or viaduct. We shall not try to fit the bridge in as an afterthought. The major features have to be settled at the planning stage, when the operating routes are related to the scenery. We build our tunnel into the framework so that it runs through a hill, or through high ground. It is always tempting to place a turnout in such a position that a train will disappear into a tunnel and emerge on either of two routes leading from the back. But a derailment in a fixed tunnel can be extremely vexing. Even when the engine has a straight run through, the tunnel should not be a long one unless we are able to reach a breakdown without disturbing the structure. Its height in OO gauge, for single-track, is 57 mm. and its width about the same. For double-track the measurements are 75 mm. and 105, allowing for a six-foot way between the inner rails of 32. On a Western Region layout the distance between the inner rails may be ten or twelve feet—shades of Isambard Kingdom Brunel—and therefore a Western Region tunnel could be made wider.

Of bridges what can be said? They come in all shapes and sizes. Hornby-Dublo, Tri-ang, Märklin, Master Models and Pocher together present a number ready-made, and it is also possible to buy an interesting kit in the Airfix range. The home-constructor uses wood or strong card and is careful to respect the scale of his layout. Measured from the rails to the underside of the span, the ordinary station foot-bridge is normally not more than fifteen feet high.

Footbridges and road bridges cross the track, but the best bridge of all is the one that carries a train. On some layouts, especially in America, a bridge of this kind is built into the supporting framework of the baseboard—usually a long narrow construction. As the bridge structure lies below the working level, a train goes over the bridge without having to climb at any point.

When the bridge stands on the baseboard, the track needs to be designed on two levels. Such an arrangement is not at all easy on a small layout, and the more we experiment the more we admire the model railway of R. A. Dalton who, with a patience possible only to a schoolmaster, built a four-level scale O gauge railway in a room thirteen feet by nine with none of the gradients exceeding three per cent and

none of the main-line curves sharper than three-foot radius; all in a rise of twenty-three inches. Advanced modellers with complicated grid frameworks wonder how it was done. A grid framework is an open-top construction which gives the modeller greater freedom to build levels, tunnels, bridges, viaducts, cuttings and embankments. The spaces are eventually boarded over—if the enthusiast ever reaches the stage when he can use them no further.

Masonry for bridges, tunnel portals and other structures is best stuck on to the cardboard or Bristol board in the form of printed sheets. Home-made brickwork may spoil an excellent model; Bilteezi, Merco or Modelcraft brick-work will turn a crude model into an apparent masterpiece. The bricks are a handy guide to dimension: we count so many up and so many across.

It is a common mistake in modelling walls to cut the card slightly and then bend it. Each cut should be complete and clean. In making a four-walled building the separate pieces of card are first joined in pairs, the front wall to one of the ends and the rear wall to the other end. Each pair is held together with parcel strip. The

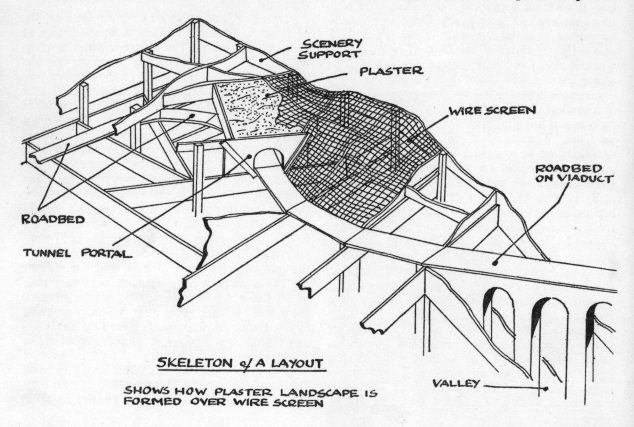

SKELETON of A LAYOUT

SHOWS HOW PLASTER LANDSCAPE IS
FORMED OVER WIRE SCREEN

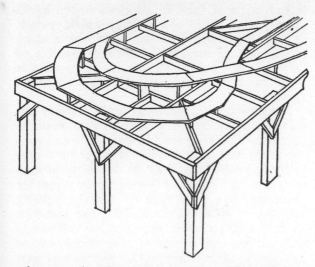

edges are then brought together, and finally the two units are assembled by the same method. When the building paper is evenly glued to the surfaces the corner bindings will be invisible.

Windows are cut out while the card is still bare. If we need to make a hole later, we cut from the finished side and remove the piece by pushing it back. A loose razor-blade is not the best tool; sooner or later the brick-work is bloodstained. Fixed into one of those little metal holders (the pencil-sharpener kind) the blade becomes much easier to use as well as safer. An X-acto knife is the choice of most modellers.

Almost every modelled countryside should have a church. The A3 church sheet is one of the most popular building papers in the Bilteezi series. Ready-made churches by Faller are fitted with lighting and with bells which ring at predetermined intervals.

Farms may be bought complete, constructed from Anorma kits, or made at home, with Bilteezi sheets D2 and D3 to transform the bare structure of card. Nearly everything that we would want on our layout can be added to it in at least one of these three ways. The range of complete purchasable articles increases rapidly. If we want to save time, we can apply Velvet Spray in various colours to give an impression of grassland, corn fields and roads, and then dot the landscapes with Tri-ang buildings or Superquick structures pressed out of stiff card.

Everyone should be aware of the charming Airfix models for OO gauge. I am not sure whether the great variety of road vehicles, from a traction engine to the latest monster with fins, makes our choice easier or difficult; but certainly we shall find what we need in the Liliput and Matchbox series and among the Dinky Toys, some of which are produced to OO scale. Quite properly, the human beings are still more numerous. Slater's Huminitures, after they have been dipped in hot water, can be moulded to any position. We should have human figures and animals in our landscape, but not too many of them. An excessive number of items, or an extreme amount of detail, harms the final impression. The problem, as in painting, is to select and omit. However rural our landscape, we may like to have some kind of industrial installation that can be served by a freight train. Oil refinery towers are obtainable from Vollmer. Those who build their own refineries may collect little plastic tubes.

In these days the textbook rules of school geography are constantly broken. Towns spring up without benefit of fords or the confluences of rivers, and a factory or a group of offices may stand almost everywhere. While we shall not erect atomic plants in the beauty spots on our layout, we need not tie a modern industry to a particular kind of area. A dairy factory or a water-mill will be in farming country, but we cannot say that a chemical factory or a laboratory will never be found near a wood or in a quiet valley. We have the same freedom with airfields, providing that the ground is level—a point to keep in mind during the planning.

It is more important to think of the products and of the loads that our trains will carry. Slater's cement bags suggest a concrete plant and Slater's sacks of flour a granary or mill. Other ideas arise from our possession of special wagons. The Tri-ang milk wagons link naturally with a dairy factory and with churns from Bradshaw, Master Models or Slater's.

Wherever a factory stands, a road will lead to it. We must not forget the highways and byways. A macadamised road may be laid as emery powder sprinkled on glue or on a black-painted surface, and a white road as granite dust or gravel on a sticky foundation. Strips of black emery paper or roofing felt are equally effective.

Loose bits of grit, or any particles that might harm the engine, must be carefully removed. For this reason I have been chary of mentioning loose track ballast in our early plans. When the scenery is in place and the general design has been fixed, cork dust or granules may be sprinkled on the glue area unless we prefer a cork strip such as Peco Underlay. A shilling bag of Elk Ballast is safer for the engine than a quantity of sand.

If track is to be laid out-of-doors for either a short or long period, the bed on which it lies should be clear of grit and bits of grass. When the running is intended to be fairly frequent so far as the weather allows, the laying of a permanent route, with tunnels and bridges (see *Garden Railways* by R. E. Tustin) will open up a new field of modelling and provide the garden with an attraction of great charm. The formation, or track bed, can be made of stones, old brick, or clinker, with a top layer of cement breeze—about one part of cement to six or seven parts of cinder. While none of the gauges below O is ideal for a garden railway, even TT is not completely unsuitable. The enthusiasm shown by cats tends to be excessive.

On winter days a developed scenic layout with a backdrop brings the bright countryside of summer into the compass of a room. Bassett-Lowke and Master Models supply painted backdrops which fit together, and Hamblings have plain scenes which the modeller colours himself. Pictures designed for educational purposes, enlarged photographs, and illustrations from magazines are often used successfully. The background need not be entirely independent of the layout. At various places in the Wild West I have seen two-storey buildings with only one floor. The imposing façade was a fake. On a model railway such trickery is justified by art, and we may virtuously carry it further with the introduction of false fronts close to the backdrop. I have heard of a railway which extends secretly into another room. Even with a more modest arrangement than this, it is possible to delay a train behind the scenes or to send it back in a manner not anticipated by the spectator.

Mechanical and electrical tricks are not unknown on layouts. If a piece of cellophane is painted with wavy lines and mounted as a rotating drum with a light inside it at the back of a cellophane waterfall, the light will show through to create an illusion of flowing water. Another effect employs a rheostat to dim the lighting gradually so that the street lights can come on in the dusk. To some, such devices will hint a little at the fairground or the shop-window novelty; to others they will be legitimately part of a hobby which has a good deal in common with the theatre if we accept a model railway as being itself a kind of illusion. Whatever our view, we must agree that night-running can be delightful, with lights in the trains, lights in buildings, signals changing colour, and the telegraph lines gleaming by the trackside. There is no finer moment in railway modelling than when a train with brightly visible headlights swings towards us from the curve of a hill.

With or without illumination, our railway looks bigger once the scenery has been laid. The trains seem to go on longer journeys, especially where the track is single. But our greater satisfaction lies in the knowledge that we are now operating, like a real railway, in an environment. The picture is complete.

CHAPTER EIGHTEEN

Line Clear Ahead

THE picture is complete; but it will never be finished. There will always be something to add, something to alter, something to improve though it means bettering perfection. Were it otherwise, the craft of railway modelling would not cast so long a spell on so many.

Even if at some time we turn towards other interests, or are pressed towards them by circumstance, the new activity may well have been inspired by the old. The railway modeller takes a camera to the lineside on sunny afternoons, and is soon a photographer. He examines buildings and discovers that architecture as a subject is far from dull. Looking for weeds to pickle and paint, he becomes aware of the beauty in a tangled hedgerow.

Modelling opens many doors. But there is also plenty to engross us within the strict field of the hobby itself. Every month three bright magazines are published in England to supply us with facts, ideas and advice. Some modellers read them all—*Model Railway News*, *Model Railway Constructor*, and *Railway Modeller*. Not a few subscribe as well, through Bradshaw's, to *Model Railroader* or *Model Trains* from America, or improve their French by taking *Loco Revue* which is distributed (with an insert in English) by Percival Marshall. Similarly, the English magazines are awaited with eagerness in countries outside the United Kingdom. The traffic is, of course, strongest within the English-speaking world and is not the smallest contribution to the friendship of its peoples. Among European countries, France has *Loco Revue*, *L'Echo du Petit Train* and *Modelisme*; the German-speaking countries *Miniaturbahnen*, *Modelleisenbahner* and *Eisenbahn-Amateur*; Italy *Italmodel Ho Rivarossi*; Spain *Tren Miniatura* and Denmark *Modelbane Nyt*.

Besides the magazines there are books. By a natural process, the modeller builds up a library. It is not confined to books about models and modelling, for an interest in miniature railways implies an interest in the real ones as well —in their operation, their history, and the men who sent the trains rolling across the world. To the excellent little railway volumes in the Globe and True Book series the beginner adds, one by one, such titles as *Railways of Britain* by Cecil J. Allen (Nelson), *Locomotives* by Brian Reed (Temple Press) and *Unusual Railways* by B. G. Wilson and J. R. Day; together with the larger studies by Hamilton Ellis, Roger Lloyd, L. T. C. Rolt, O. S. Nock and G. Freeman Allen whose *British Railways To-day and To-morrow* (Ian Allan) provides an exciting picture of the great changes now in progress. Out-of-print volumes come to be treasured, and the enthusiast knows the sweet pleasure of running down, in some dim bookshop, a rarity that he had thought would elude him for ever.

Whatever concerns the modeller in the exercise of his hobby is very important to him indeed.

*   *   *

How many passengers can tell the speed of a train when they are riding in it? Like most other people, the model railwayman knows that the train makes a kind of thump whenever it passes over the joint between two lengths of rail. Unlike most others, he also knows that there are twenty-two of these joints in every mile. By counting the thumps, with his eyes on a watch, he can therefore calculate the distance travelled in a certain time.

Because of his hobby, he may also know what the engine is saying when it whistles. He may think, too, of Casey Jones who made his whistle sing like the whippoorwill along the

Salt Lake Line until the sad wet night when, driving like the devil's hounds—

So turn on your water and shovel in your coal
Stick your head out of the window, watch those
drivers roll ...

he crashed into the rear of another train and died with his hand on the throttle.

It was through a smaller crash than Casey's that engines were first given a voice. On the fourth of May in 1833 a market cart loaded with eighty dozen eggs and fifty pounds of butter arrived on a level crossing at exactly the same time as George Stephenson's *Samson*. Distressed by so much scrambled egg on the track, Ashlen Bagster, manager of the Leicester and Swannington, suggested that Stephenson might fit an engine with a horn that could be blown by steam. Ten days later a maker of musical instruments brought Stephenson a steam trumpet shaped like a megaphone. It gave forth a note similar to the new sound on our railways, the toot of the diesel-electric.

From the days of the pioneer wood-burners, the engine whistle has been especially familiar in America. The first trains shrieked. Besides frightening the Indians, their unearthly whoops were so distressing to old ladies and little children that a new device, the bull whistle, was eventually introduced together with chime whistles of a kind long used on river boats. A newspaper editor expressed the fear that cattle would now be lured on to the line instead of being scared off. Less enthusiastic than these music-loving cows were the prairie farmers living within calling distance of a locomotive whose whistle stuck one day during the last war. It remained stuck for hours and there was panic on the prairie.

Once you are interested in trains it is surprising what you can discover about train whistles.

* * *

There used to be a train in Cornwall which, whenever it was late, delayed other trains all the way up to the north of Scotland. The first train affected was the mail from Penzance to Exeter. If the single-line was not clear, the mail had to wait. This meant a corresponding delay for the mail from Exeter to Bristol. The Bristol mail to Crewe then had to be kept back, and the mail from Crewe to Carlisle was late in turn, with a similar effect on trains from Carlisle to Edinburgh, from Edinburgh to Perth and from Perth

to Inverness. Single track on the last stage then swung the chain reaction back again towards Cornwall. It took two days for the process to cease.

Could there be a better illustration of how a railway works as a unified system with each of its parts affecting the whole? The model railwayman knows this from his own operations on the layout.

* * *

It is as a system that the railway will be studied and admired in the future. Ever since the Rocket performed at Rainhill, the hero of the piece has naturally been the locomotive. But as the Age of Steam draws to an end, the focus of interest is changing from the engine to the permanent way. The diesel-electric, for all its mechanical excellence, excites little affection, and the atomic locomotive of to-morrow is more likely to be admired than liked.

Fortunately this is not the only change, or the railway might soon lose its romantic appeal and be taken for granted like the bus services. The end of one age is the beginning of another. With modernization, and particularly with the increasing use of remote-control, the railway itself becomes interesting as a system—a great machine geared to the world's work and pleasure. On the mile-long trains of America the guards and drivers talk by radio, and in big railway stations the passenger's seat is booked by television.

So far there has been little or no fall in the affection felt for the steam engine. On the contrary, older people tend to value it more, as a familiar thing which is beginning to pass. But the next generation or so may well bring a difference. At present the steam engine still exists. Whether it will have much interest when it can seldom be seen is extremely doubtful. The six-year-olds already talk of diesels. For them, as they grow up, the diesels will have been there always, like television.

The model railwayman is ready for natural change. In a sense he has anticipated it, not only with his miniature diesels and all-electric locomotives but also and more strongly in his regard for remote-control, scenery, and the whole pattern of railway operation.

* * *

I was in the cab of the first British main-line diesel when the white-coated driver took his seat at the controls for the maiden run at Newton-le-Willows. In the great Vulcan Foundry of Robert Stephenson the clangour ceased; and then the sudden hush was shattered by a triumphant blast from the two-tone horn as the new locomotive glided out into the sunshine. Perhaps the sound rang across Chat Moss where George Stephenson laid the tracks of the world's first true passenger railway. At any rate it was, to all of us there, a voice of the future signalling confidently to the past.

In America the change has been sharper. Whereas in 1924 about sixty-five thousand steam locomotives were chuffing and roaring on the railways of the United States, the total is now only a few thousand, and most of these are on the quieter lines or working out their last days at mines and quarries. By an irony which many live-steamers will appreciate, the latest stream-lined engines were the first to go.

Happily, the departing heroes are being treated with respect. It is clearly impossible, as the keenest live-steamer must realize, for the railways to make a museum-piece of every discarded engine, and we must be content if here and there a veteran is set aside to represent the others.

This was the course taken by the Pennsylvania Railroad, which extends for 10,285 route-miles, after Locomotive No. 1361, a K-4 of 1918, had made her last run. At a dedication ceremony of the famous Horseshoe Curve in the Appalachians the children of the railway city of Altoona took over the old engine as a memorial.

The active life of No. 1361 was much shorter than that of *Smoky Mary*, the Stephenson locomotive which ran in Louisiana for a hundred years. But in about a third of that time No. 1361 steamed 2,469,000 miles, equal to nearly a hundred trips around the world. The man who drove her on the last miles was John P. Murphy. "Steamers," he said, "were always like something alive."

*   *   *

Steam engines were like something alive—and still are, wherever they operate. The smaller their size the more endearing we find them. For the railway modeller, a holiday may mean a trip on one of the miniature lines such as the Romney, Hythe and Dymchurch, the Ravenglass and Eskdale in Cumberland or one of those in Wales.

Many people visit Wales expressly to ride on the Festiniog and the Talyllyn railways. Down the coast, not far below Aberystwyth, British Railways run their Vale of Rheidol train with three small 2-6-2 tank engines. As the train winds higher and higher above the Vale to Devil's Bridge, the driver opens his cylinder cocks to warn the hill sheep.

Within the same tour the visitor may easily include the ascent of Snowdon behind a tall-stacked engine on the mountain railway. He will also want to go up to the Great Orme, that huge mass of carboniferous limestone between Conway Bay and Llandudno. Every summer a hundred thousand passengers are wound to the summit and down again by the two colliery-type engines of the Llandudno Cable Railway.

Full of interest, too, are many of the more conventional railways—the old Somerset and Dorset, for example and the Whitby and Pickering, begun in 1833 after a report had been made by George Stephenson. There is no better way of entering Wales, or leaving it, than by the route of the old Cambrian Railways.

*   *   *

Such journeys call for a camera. The railway modeller collects pictures—photographs of his own, magazine illustrations and old prints when they come his way. He also likes to have a few antique or unusual train tickets in his special drawer. Sometimes he becomes a collector of magazine back-numbers and is delighted when he picks up the long-missing issue which will complete his set for 1935.

Old timetables delight him. He notes that the shortest time between Paddington and Oxford in 1888 was an hour and eighteen minutes, compared with an hour and twelve minutes more than seventy years later. Canon Roger Lloyd tells us in *The Fascination of Railways* that when William Temple, future Archbishop of Canterbury, was Headmaster of Repton he would produce a copy of Bradshaw's Railway Guide and order an offender to find out, as an imposition, the quickest and best way of travelling from, perhaps, Great Yarmouth to Exeter without touching London. "The boy had to write down all the changes, and the times of arrival and departure at every point of change. When the imposition was shown-up, Temple would look at it with an expert eye, and would often tell him that he knew a better way of doing the journey."

For a boy railway modeller this would not be a punishment. It would be fun.

*   *   *

Above all the railway enthusiast keeps his eyes open. He learns to look. In the Midland goods station next to St. Pancras he notices that the bricks are of different sizes, the largest at the bottom of a wall and the smallest at the top. This was the idea of Sir Gilbert Scott who designed the Albert Memorial.

A small discovery often opens a new field of interest to the modeller. He may easily become a student of railway architecture. Many railway works are noble feats of both architecture and engineering. A Brunel or Telford viaduct takes nothing from the valley that it spans, but adds its own majestic grace to the beauty that was always there.

Little antique things constantly catch the eye. I doubt whether one can still see, as one could some years ago, a notice in old Great Western carriages telling the thirsty passenger that the guard or stationmaster would be pleased to sell him a bottle of claret, price one shilling. But there are plenty of other details not unlike this in the charm of their unexpectedness.

*   *   *

Again and again the railway-lover knows the pleasure of opening a book and coming upon the description of a train journey. The book may be a novel. From *Dombey and Son* to *Doctor Zhivago* and one or two of the latest thrillers, the trains of fiction must have travelled across thousands of pages and more miles than the old K-4.

They must also have steamed along hundreds of miles of celluloid. When Edison wanted to break away from the prize-fights and horse-races which were the favourite themes of the earliest films, he realized the dramatic effect that a train would be sure to have upon the audiences. The result was *The Great Express Robbery*, adapted from a stage play of the time. It thrilled thousands; and how many millions have been thrilled since by the other trains on their thunderous way across the screen?

Such films as *The Great Locomotive Chase*, *The Big Land*, *The Spirit of St. Louis*, *Berlin Express* and *North West Frontier* are a few among the great numbers in which trains have a part. In *The Big Land* Alan Ladd persuades the Texas cattle men to bring their herds to the rail-way which his friend is building from Kansas City; and in *Berlin Express* someone has smuggled a bomb on board. Quite different from either of these is *The Titfield Thunderbolt*, a delightful English comedy and a great favourite with model railway and model engineering clubs.

The old *Inyo* engine, bought by Paramount in 1937, has showed her steam valiantly in *Dodge City*, *Rails into Laramie*, *Carson City*, *The Harvey Girls* and *Duel in the Sun*. Her fellow star, the *William Mason*, has been converted from wood to coal but has not yet achieved engine-brakes. She has plenty to do in *Wells Fargo*.

There are few interests which extend into so many territories as railway modelling. The enthusiast is never really far from his hobby. Lazing on a deck at sea, he can pick up Archie Robertson's *Slow Train to Yesterday* (Houghton Mifflin) or Stuart Legg's anthology *The Railway Book* (Rupert Hart-Davis), or *On the Old Lines*, by Peter Allen (Cleaver-Hume) and feel that they are complementary to the technical books by such expert modellers as John W. Ahern, Edward Beal, Ernest F. Carter and P. R. Wickham.

*   *   *

A long time ago I went to see *Night Mail* with Harry Watt who made it. I have never forgotten this film. Here was a romantic drama performed by ordinary people in the normal course of duty, an adventure that took place every night while most of us were asleep. The mail train rushing along in the dark with the letters that would plop through thousands of front doors in the morning; the bags dropping into the trap-net; the men at work in sorting cars; the stir of life at stations on the way: through the talents of Harry Watt, Basil Wright, Cavalcanti and W. H. Auden, these scenes from the living world became as thrilling as the best-staged train robbery in a Western. The snatching of the mail-bags at speed provided far more tension than the climax of *High Noon*.

Moving through a countryside at dawn, a train can be as beautiful as anything that man has made. We see this in *Night Mail*; and while we enjoy the visual excitements of the journey, Cavalcanti gives us the sounds—the varying rhythm of wheels on metal, the clang and clatter of buffers, the voices of railwaymen, and, uniting the whole, the verse commentary by W. H. Auden spoken to the beat of the pistons.

We may now hear these sounds at home. Discs by Transacord and others enable us to switch on a real railway as authentic atmosphere for our own busy line. Those who would like American recordings may obtain them through the Readers' Service of the Kalmbach magazines at 1027 N. 7th Street, Miwaukee 3, Wisconsin. Many of them pay tribute to an almost vanished era, as we realize from such titles as *Steam in Twilight, Farewell to Steam, Steam in Colorado* and *The Fading Giant*. They are all bargains in noise.

What I have said in an earlier chapter about sound-deadening will appear rather silly to the person who wants to operate his trains in the roar of the *Big Boy*. Another and more adaptable method of bringing sound to the layout involves the use of a Telex miniature loudspeaker with a tape-recorder or record-player connected to the rails so that the sound from the recording comes out of the locomotive unit. As the Telex Mini-mike 100 is only an inch square by three-quarters of an inch deep, it will fit into a tender. After the speaker has been wired in series with two small condensers, one side is brought into contact with the rails through the wheels of the tender and the other side through the wheels of the engine.

Railway modelling is an old hobby which refreshes itself from what is new. It seizes upon plastics, draws in the record-player and tape-recorder, and is already using the printed circuit and transistorized control.

*   *   *

All day and all night long the trains are moving. They weave in and out of the capitals of Europe. They roll through the bright air of the Andes at altitudes where oxygen has to be carried. They thunder along the trails of the vanished bison, for where the herds roved the land was flattest. They rumble through the new Wild West of Siberia. They shake the great roof of Paddington and the buns under the glass dome in the refreshment room at Mugby Junction.

Our model trains are moving too. "Bole, Tritton, Spavin Delawarr, Knipswich for Timpany. ..." "Kettle Creek, Topton, Applejack, Smoky Mountain and Cascade. ..." All over the world the little trains wind their way from station to station and into the affections of the young and the young-at-heart.

TWIN-RUNNING **TRIX**

See the Revolutionary

BO-BO
ELECTRIC LOCOMOTIVE

A 'must' for every enthusiast

26010

TRIX OVERHEAD CATENARY SYSTEM

The Trix catenary system is designed to give maximum realism combined with simple fitting and efficient operation. It can be used in conjunction with any track on fixed layouts where an overhead supply is required.

The support post can be attached to Trix track by means of the special clip.
Extension pieces are available for joining two posts to extend over a double track.
The simple wire joining clip enables crossings and branches to be made at any desired point.

This superb model will, by simple adjustment of the shoes, run on two or three-rail track with or without catenary. By use of the overhead catenary it gives three-train running under individual control. The pantograph is electrically connected and is fully spring-loaded to take all variations in height of overhead wires. The Bo-Bo is fitted with fully operative headlights and cab light for maximum realism.

TRIX TRIX TWIN RAILWAYS,
308 SUMMER LANE, BIRMINGHAM

TRIX FOR ALL AGES

The ever-popular, powerful
BRITANNIA

finished in B.R. Green - With full detail!

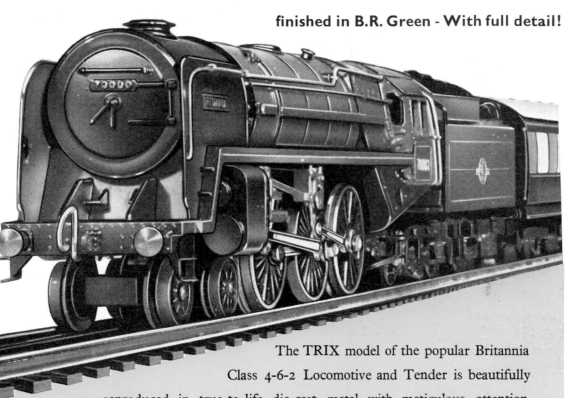

The TRIX model of the popular Britannia Class 4-6-2 Locomotive and Tender is beautifully reproduced in true-to-life die-cast metal with meticulous attention to detail. Finished in British Railways Green. Powerfully engined, it is capable of the tractive effort necessary for hauling long, realistic trains.

TRIX TWIN RAILWAYS, 308 SUMMER LANE, BIRMINGHAM

ROBUST **TRIX**

The reliable, versatile three

1 **CLASS V** ▶

4-6-0 Class 5 Locomotive is a "fine workhorse". A versatile addition to any enthusiast's equipment, this finely detailed Trix model will be equally at home—and equally authentic—heading passenger or goods trains. It is available in black or British Railways Green livery.

◀ **0-6-2 TANK** **2**

0-6-2 Class 66 xx W.R. Tank Loco is Trix faithful reproduction of its British Railways counterpart. The die-cast shell is fully detailed and is correctly lined and finished. Available in British Railways Green livery.

3 **RUSTON HORNSBY DIESEL SHUNTER** ▶

Trix Ruston Hornsby Diesel Shunter is fully detailed, finished in authentic green and silver, and supplied complete with grey shunter's truck. This is a "must" for your shunting yard.

TRIX

TRIX TWIN RAILWAYS, 308 SUMMER LANE, BIRMINGHAM

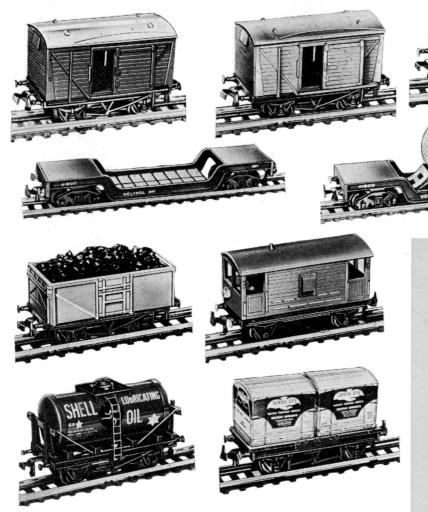

TRIX VERSATILE TRACK

At last! TRAINS ARE RUNNING SMOOTHLY
with Trix Twin Universal Points

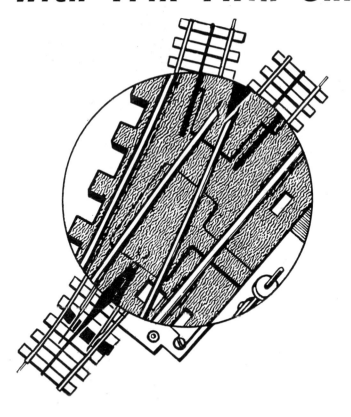

Inter-runnning between systems
is no problem with TRIX
Universal Points and the NEW
TRIX track and pointwork will
take the locos and rolling stock
of all OO Systems.

U.727 Universal points hand
operated
(left or right hand).

U.728 Universal points remote
controlled
(left or right hand).

TRIX TWIN RAILWAYS, 308 SUMMER LANE, BIRMINGHAM

TRIX ENDS THE PERFECT LAYOUT

Bring your layout up to date!

TRIX STATIONS

Trix Twin Railways Manyways Stations add so much more scope to your layout. There are six complete sets available and all units are interchangeable and can be obtained separately allowing an infinite variety of combinations. With **Manyways Units** no station ever becomes obsolete. All units are built to the same scale in very strong die-cast metal and are superbly finished in imitation concrete.

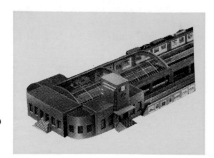

TRIX TWIN TRACK

By adding step-by-step to your standard 14-piece oval you can make up any of the eight fascinating layouts, fully illustrated in the TRIX current catalogue. Altogether 30 different pieces of track are included in these sets.

TRIX ACCESSORIES

Trix continuously add new interesting true-to-life items to their range of accessories. You are offered many fascinating Loads and Containers, Track and Lineside Accessories, Yard signal and signal box switches, switches for operating points magnetic rail, remote uncouplers etc.

TRIX

TRIX TWIN RAILWAYS, 308 SUMMER LANE, BIRMINGHAM

№165 S⁴ Buck